When Charles Timoney and his French wife were both made redundant in the same week they decided to try living in France for a year or so. It proved much harder than expected. Charles' O-level in French was little help when everyone around him consistently used a wide variety of impenetrable slang and persisted in the annoying habit of talking about things he had never heard of. But they stayed. Two decades and two thoroughly French children later, he decided to write the book that would have saved him from so many blunders and misunderstandings along the way. This is it.

A Certain...

Je Ne Sais Quoi

THE IDEAL GUIDE TO

Sounding, ACTING

AND *Shrugging*

LIKE THE FRENCH

PENGUIN BOOKS

PENGUIN BOOKS

Published by the Penguin Group
Penguin Books Ltd, 80 Strand, London WC2R ORL, England
Penguin Group (USA) Inc., 375 Hudson Street, New York, New York 10014, USA
Penguin Group (Canada), 90 Eglinton Avenue East, Suite 700, Toronto, Ontario, Canada M4P 2Y3
(a division of Pearson Penguin Canada Inc.)
Penguin Ireland, 25 St Stephen's Green, Dublin 2, Ireland (a division of Penguin Books Ltd)
Penguin Group (Australia), 250 Camberwell Road, Camberwell, Victoria 3124, Australia
(a division of Pearson Australia Group Pty Ltd)
Penguin Books India Pvt Ltd, 11 Community Centre, Panchsheel Park, New Delhi – 110 017, India
Penguin Group (NZ), 67 Apollo Drive, Rosedale, North Shore 0632,
New Zealand (a division of Pearson New Zealand Ltd)
Penguin Books (South Africa) (Pty) Ltd, 24 Sturdee Avenue,
Rosebank, Johannesburg 2196, South Africa

Penguin Books Ltd, Registered Offices: 80 Strand, London WC2R ORL, England

www.penguin.com

First published 2009
4

Copyright © Charles Timoney, 2009
Illustrations © Vincent Burgeon, 2009
All rights reserved

The moral right of the author has been asserted

Set in Linotype Sabon
Typeset by Rowland Phototypesetting Ltd, Bury St Edmunds, Suffolk
Printed in England by Clays Ltd, St Ives plc

ISBN: 978-0-141-04167-4

www.greenpenguin.co.uk

Penguin Books is committed to a sustainable future
for our business, our readers and our planet.
The book in your hands is made from paper
certified by the Forest Stewardship Council.

For my parents

'. . . as this fellow is a Frenchman, we all realise that it is only a question of time before something dastardly occurs.'

Frenchman's Creek, Daphne du Maurier, 1941

Contents

Acknowledgements

Thanks are principally due to Georgina Laycock and Jane Turnbull – how anyone manages to publish a book without them is a mystery to me.

I would also like to thank those who provided support, encouragement, suggestions, ideas and corrections for this book and the previous one, including in no particular order: Peter and Helen, Polly and Mark, Peter and Raija, Siggi and Christine, Béatrice and Jean-François, Andy Kay for his reviews, and my colleagues, who, wittingly or not, answered all my questions, notably Laurence for les enfants; also Anne for the history, Marc for the sport, Valérie for the cheese, Nathalie for successfully predicting the outcome, Eric and, of course, Inès, Sarah and Sebastian.

Introduction

A few months ago, having tried all sorts of things to cure a sore back, I thought I would go and see a healer.

Much laying-on of hands not only cured my back, it revealed the healer to be something of a medium.

'I can feel that at some point in your life you had a long, painful and deeply traumatic experience. What's more, I can now clearly see that it happened when you were about twenty-eight or thirty,' she surprised me by exclaiming while putting the finishing touches to my back.

'But what kind of experience could produce internal scars like these?' she went on, clearly appalled by the depths of suffering that she had unearthed in one so apparently carefree.

From the dates she gave, it could only be one thing. I remembered it all too well: it had indeed been long, painful and deeply traumatic.

'That was the time I came to live in France.'

Not wishing you to go through the same traumatic experience, I thought I would share with you here the hard-won knowledge of all those years in France.

In my earlier book, *Pardon My French*, I gave definitions for various useful words that I wish I had known when I first came to live in France. While those words will help you understand a lot of what you see and hear around you, there is much more that you could usefully know.

I have kept the idea of key words but, rather than just defining them, I have used them in themes to illustrate various aspects of

French life: a typical French day, how to get the best out of restaurants and bars, the perils of greeting people, a beginner's guide to gesticulating and more.

Pardon My French showed how to unleash your inner Gaul. However, in order to refine your inner Gaul, to enjoy France more and, hopefully, to avoid being spotted as a tourist too quickly, you will need that little extra – that certain *je ne sais quoi*. This book should help you find it.

1. Une journée française – a typical day

However high your standard of living in the UK may be, there is something which stops you from living the true Good Life. For there is something lacking in your life, a thing that is almost omnipresent in France.

This thing forms an essential part of French daily routine. It marks both the start of the day (which is why we are starting with it here) and also the end of it. Were you somehow able to snap your fingers and make it disappear throughout France, the sense of loss would be overwhelming and, I am convinced, the majority of people would simply not be able to make it through the following day.

But what can this key element of French life be? Wine? Cheese? Sex??

It is something far more important than all of those: I am referring to *les volets* – shutters.

Practically all dwellings in France, from the simplest studio to the most opulent château, have windows fitted with shutters. Shutting and, more importantly, opening the shutters is an essential French way of expressing the simple joy of living.

You don't have to take my word for this; you just have to watch French adverts on TV.

Any advert for coffee, or breakfast cereal, or for that most curious of French breakfast drinks, *Ricoré* (a chicory-based milky drink that tastes better than it sounds), starts with an attractive, happy and smiling parent pushing open the shutters to greet a new, sunny day before going to prepare breakfast for their attractive, happy and smiling family.

Of course, shutters come in many guises – metal ones that you fold back in sections or plastic ones that you roll up by winding a crank handle that hangs by the window, or an electric version of this which always strikes me as cheating – but the real shutter, the true shutter of breakfast adverts is a simple painted wooden pair that you open from the inside and push back simultaneously against the wall. It is, of course, absolutely crucial to smile winningly while doing so or the day will get off to a very bad start indeed.

Opening and closing your shutters should preferably be done at the same time every day. You open them as soon as you are awake, to greet the day and to allow your neighbours to see you in your nightclothes with your face marked by sleep. This is a key moment in their day too. In the evening comes another communal moment: as soon as it starts to get dark, everyone sets about closing their shutters in unison.

The sound of shutters being opened or closed is thus a fundamental feature of communal living in France.

Shutter opening is an example of the ways in which a French day differs from one elsewhere. And now, a kind of appetizer to the rest of the book, I am going to look briefly at a few daily events that seem peculiar to France.

LA COUETTE

Having opened your shutters and smiled cheerfully at the new day, you might reasonably assume that you are now free to go and have your breakfast. Unfortunately, there is one more thing to do first.

Now that the window and the shutters are open you are able

to take the second step in a French day: showing the neighbours your bedding.

A surprising number of French people, even those who live in inner-city flats, are clearly convinced that you have to air your bedding every morning. Thus, as soon as the sound of clattering shutters from next door has died away, you are treated to a series of effortful grunts as *les couettes* – quilts – are heaved off beds and hung out of the window.

It is all surprisingly intimate: you see your neighbours in their pyjamas, T-shirt or nightdress, you are amused at what they look like before they have brushed their hair, and you gain a fascinating insight into their taste in quilt covers and pillowcases and how often they wash them. It is something which I do not generally see in the week but which I enjoy to the full at weekends. Our neighbours currently favour blue quilts with sailing boats on them.

France being a country where romantic assignations are not unknown (though, I suppose, this is true of many countries), it appears that you can even use quilt-airing as a code. Hanging it out of the window in a special way, or at a particular time, can be agreed to mean, 'The coast is clear' – now is a good time for a lover to drop round.

UNE BOUTEILLE D'EAU

The average French person consumes a huge quantity of bottled mineral water. Of course, you knew that, but bear with me as I am really just leading up to the next topic.

Mineral water bottles are found in every home but they are also extremely common at work: the majority of office workers seem to have a plastic mineral water bottle on their desk at all times. In most cases people will buy the day's bottle of water on the way to work. However, as many offices now provide chilled water dispensers many people just keep a bottle on their desk and go along and fill it up at the dispenser whenever necessary.

All this means that there are always an awful lot of plastic mineral water bottles about the place. Which brings me handily on to the next topic.

LES BOUCHONS

From the preceding paragraphs, we have seen that the average French person buys a huge amount of plastic bottles in the course of a year. With all the current interest in the environment, you may wonder whether any of these bottles are recycled.

Well, they are; at least, partially.

If you imagine a plastic bottle of water you will see that it comprises a large and voluminous bottle and a small, compact screw top. Faced with such a combination, and asked to recycle just one of the components, you would very probably concentrate on the bottle part and be prepared to sacrifice the top.

However, in the building where I work, and in plenty of buildings like it, there are special bins provided to allow employees to recycle part of their plastic water bottles. But, for reasons that I have never been able to explain, these bins are only intended for *les bouchons* – the plastic bottle tops.

Whether at home or in the office, the majority of employees religiously save their bottle tops and, when they have acquired a good stock, they take a plastic bag of multicoloured tops to the recycling bin and proudly pour them in. Occasionally there are bottle-top collections organized for charity where each bottle top collected results in a fixed sum of money – one centime or so – being given to the cause in question. Participation in these events borders on the fanatical with people pestering their friends and neighbours to save their tops so as to be able to submit a huge bag of the things.

The bottles themselves are just thrown in the bin.

It is all very odd.

AU DÉJEUNER

At lunchtime in France, not only is food eaten, it is also talked about. In fact, French people talk about food constantly. At any moment, whether it is during a coffee break or at lunch at the canteen, someone will suddenly start talking about meals they have eaten or those that they are planning to eat. With the least prompting anyone will describe, in minute detail, the food they had at a restaurant the night before and speculate on the recipes used. No one listening will find this in any way odd: rather they are more than likely to ask for even more details. This sort of conversation makes me feel dizzy: it also makes me hungry.

I had lunch the other day at the canteen with three male colleagues, all in their late twenties or early thirties, and all single. Did we talk about football? Or about the pretty new student who had just come to spend a few weeks in our department? Or even about the latest political scandal to shake the country? No. We talked about *salade niçoise*. The three blokes (for I didn't say much) spent a good twenty minutes having a sometimes quite heated discussion about what were, or were not, the essential ingredients of a *salade niçoise*. One mentioned rice at one point and was met with a veritable barrage of contempt from the other two. 'Rice!' they sneered. 'In a *salade niçoise*? Are you having a laugh?' I had been on the point of entering the discussion by suggesting black olives, but suddenly decided to engross myself in my fruit salad rather than risk a similar rebuke.

The meal ended peacefully enough, but with some outstanding disagreements. Ten minutes after getting back to our respective desks an email arrived from one of the three, addressed to us all. It contained a recipe, from an unimpeachable source, for a true *salade niçoise*. There was indeed no rice.

LES MÉDICAMENTS

If you were suddenly transported into an unknown office and told to determine whether the office was in Britain or in France, all you would have to do would be to open the top desk drawer. If you found a newspaper, a cycle light with a flat battery, some peppermints or a couple of chocolate digestive biscuits, you could be sure the office was British. If, on the other hand, you found at least two sorts of medicine, it would be clear that you were in France.

The French take a lot of *médicaments* – medicines – and they very often take them at lunchtime. And they don't do it discreetly. If there are pills to be taken they will produce a selection of blister packs, ostentatiously pop out pills and capsules and then loudly swallow them. There is rarely any attempt to hide the name of the drug on the packaging. In any case, this would be a waste of time because you are always treated to some kind of explanation such as '*Je dois prendre mes antibiotiques*' – I have to take my antibiotics.

But if you want to look really French at mealtimes, taking a few antibiotics won't be enough. You have to produce a glass phial or two. Medicines in little glass tubes are relatively unknown in Britain. In France they are everywhere. Assuming that you are having lunch with someone who is over forty, the chances of being treated to the glass phial show are high. With no explanation or warning, your lunch partner will produce one or more glass tubes from a handbag or pocket. Such tubes come in two basic types: a smallish one with thin, stick-like projections at both ends, and a slightly larger version with a single, tapering neck. If it is the first one, its owner will pour a glass of water, crack off one of the sticks, hold the broken end over the glass and then crack off the other end. Breaking off the second end lets the air in and allows the liquid to flow out into the glass, where it is mixed carefully with the water and drunk. The broken sticks and the phial are then dumped in the ashtray whereupon you spend the rest of the meal trying to read the name of the drug written on the side.

The bigger phials with a single end are more complicated as you can't usually crack the end off unaided. Your friend will therefore rummage around in the box in search of a tiny file to saw the neck of the phial before cracking it dramatically into the glass.

If you are planning on taking a phial or two at mealtimes to try to look a bit French, it is as well to practise the filing part of the operation beforehand as it can prove quite tricky.

AU MARCHÉ

At some point in the day, many French people visit their local market.

Despite the power of the supermarkets, the local market is still an important part of people's daily lives. A surprising number of towns and villages, as well as districts of major cities, have a market a couple of times a week, usually on a weekday as well as at the weekend. Even our village of five thousand inhabitants has a market on Tuesdays and Saturdays which has stalls covering the essentials of life: a butcher, a fishmonger, fruit and veg stalls and a cheese shop. It is a key part of village life: residents of all ages would be completely lost if it ever closed. The bigger the community, the bigger the market with the essential range of stalls being supplemented by bakers, flower sellers and stalls selling pulses and olives. While most markets are temporary and are set up on the market square the night before, the bigger ones have at least a part held inside a permanent structure. The big market at Versailles, for example, has four imposing market buildings set at the corners of the market square, the square being filled with stalls on market days. The quality of food is almost always good, and value for money in all but the most fashionable markets is excellent. But if you want a real bargain, you have to wait till the very end when the stallholders are getting ready to pack up. This is when they call out to you as you go past, offering irresistible last-minute bargains.

But the important thing, the really important thing about markets, is that they are generally held on car parks. This means that if you arrive somewhere late in the evening and find a parking spot that seems too good to be true, beware! Parking the night before a market is a sure-fire way of having your car towed away. The only thing worse than stumbling out of a hotel first thing in the morning to find a fruit and veg stall on the spot where you left your car is to get up to find that market stalls have been erected on every square metre of the market square except on those occupied by your car. Believe me, there is nothing more forlorn-looking than a single, lonely Peugeot surrounded by a sea of unfriendly stallholders.

LE TAXI

While taking a taxi is not necessarily a daily event, I thought that the subject deserved a mention, and here is as good a time in the day as any.

In London, taxi drivers have to show a thorough mastery of the city streets by taking a searching exam known as 'The Knowledge'. In Paris, the principle is similar. However, it is the passenger who is expected to have the mastery of the city streets, not the driver. This is because the driver is very often a complete stranger to the city and generally appears lost. In the old days, this wasn't a problem: if you knew where you wanted to go, you showed the taxi driver the way, he listened politely, took you where you wanted to go and everything was fine. If you wanted to go somewhere new, either you or the driver had to have a good map and at least one of you had to know how to read it. We once asked a Parisian taxi driver to take us to Versailles. He looked a bit alarmed but said it shouldn't really be a problem because he had a map. As soon as I saw it I realized that things were not going to go well because it was the big Michelin map of France. I could see Toulouse, Grenoble and Perpignan, but Versailles was too small to be shown.

Nowadays, things are much more difficult because of GPS. As taxi drivers don't know where they are they all invest in a GPS. This is where the problems start because as soon as you get in the car the driver will set off dramatically in a random direction and then, after a kilometre or so, ask you to spell the name of the place where you want to go. All interest in the road in front will be abandoned and the driver will concentrate entirely, and usually unsuccessfully, on trying to type in the name of your destination. The average taxi driver is very stubborn about using his GPS and will resolutely ignore any directions you may offer, despite your assurances that you are going home and know the way blindfold.

Incidentally, Paris taxis have four fare levels – A, B, C and D – which are shown on the meter and on little coloured lights on the roof under the word 'Taxi'. A is the cheapest and is for day-time trips in central Paris. B is for night-time trips in central Paris while C and D are respectively day and night fares to a destination outside Paris. If you ever take a taxi out of Paris you will see the driver change to a higher fare level as soon as he gets beyond the Périphérique. If you think you have been spotted as a tourist, it is as well to be vigilant about the fare level shown on the meter.

FAIRE LA NAVETTE

There is a clear difference between the outward and the home-ward journeys of those who *faire la navette* – commute – on public transport in Paris. In the morning, the coach will be quiet with everyone blearily trying to read one of the free newspapers, such as *20 Minutes*, that are distributed at stations. On their return journey, having finished the paper that morning and having nothing else to read, many people pass the time by vainly trying not to eat bread.

Bread, and by this I really mean *une baguette*, is still a vital part of French culture: I have heard many people over the years declare that they could not envisage eating supper without some fresh bread to go with it. If such people don't have a baker near their home they have to buy their baguette on the way from work to the station. The chances are thus quite high that when you collapse into your seat for the Métro journey home, you will be driven to distraction by the enticing smell of fresh bread coming from nearby. If you look around, you will most likely spot two cut halves of a fresh baguette peeping out of a bag. They will have been cut by the baker so that they take up less room in the bag. If you look again a few minutes later, one of the cut ends will have disappeared leaving a jagged tear. The time taken to tear the end off a baguette and eat it is a function of the hunger, but especially the willpower, of the person carrying it. Very, very few baguette carriers reach their stop with their bread untouched.

LES INFORMATIONS

Watching the evening news – *les informations* – on TV is another key part of a typical French day. There are two main channels that offer a half-hour evening news programme – Channels 1 and 2. Each programme has its own characteristics and, more importantly, its own regular newsreader and thus each has its own devoted following. The following really is devoted – everyone seems to have their preferred channel and few people appear to vary their choice at all. The choice seems at least partly hereditary: if asked, many people admit that they watch a given channel because it is the one their parents watched (and probably still watch).

The question of choice is important because you don't pick one or other of the programmes as a function of convenience: it is not a question of preferring to watch the early evening news rather than the news at ten. This is for the simple reason that both main news programmes are on at the same time every day – 8 p.m. While this may not be that convenient, it does at least mean that whichever one you pick, most of France will be watching at the same time as you. You may find this thought comforting.

As one brought up on British TV where the six o'clock news starts every day on the stroke of six and ends, every day, at the advertised time, French news came as a bit of a surprise. Not only are both main programmes on at the same time, their start times, and more especially, their finishing times, seem somewhat variable. If you are planning on watching the eight o'clock news you should plan on it starting some time around eight-ish: it may be a minute or so before eight, or a minute or so after eight, or even, occasionally, at exactly eight o'clock. This explains why there is no clock shown on the screen, even less the striking of a clock.

There is also a similar situation at lunchtime with both main channels offering their own one o'clock news programme. I have no idea what these programmes are like for most of the year but I have very strong views on what they are like during the summer holidays. The summer holiday period is definitely the 'silly season' when it comes to the lunchtime news. Every day, international dramas are forgotten while you are treated to endearing stories of hot holidaymakers cavorting in fountains, or a report on a kind old lady who knits sun hats for elderly donkeys, or a farmer near Toulouse who has a singing goat.

It takes an especially destructive earthquake somewhere to knock a singing goat off the lunchtime headlines.

LA SOIRÉE

A French evening in front of the TV comprises two essential elements: the 8 p.m. evening news programme and the film. All the major channels show a film at around 8.45 almost every evening. As with the news, the time of the beginning of the film is somewhat vague. It is never clear what time the news will end, nor how long the following weather forecast will last. Then comes the longest series of adverts that you will ever have seen in your life before there can be any question of the film starting. But there is always a film. Most of the year it will be a film that hasn't been shown too often. In July and August it will be a film that everyone knows by heart because it is shown every summer and again at Christmas. No one seems to find this in any way frustrating: they just watch the film for the seventeenth time, and laugh in all the right places.

LE BIDET

We shall end this chapter on a note of uncertainty.

Everyone has seen a bidet.

In any true French bathroom there will be a typical bidet – one of the cream-coloured ones with that wonderful, slightly cracked finish to the glaze which only comes from old age. It won't have taps and a nozzle like those on a sink: the nozzle will be concealed so that the water flows unseen into a kind of recess which goes round the edge of the bidet, a bit like the rim round a lavatory bowl. This means that when you turn the water on, it appears miraculously, apparently from nowhere, accompanied by strange bubbling and hissing noises. With luck, the bidet will have one of those mechanical arrangements which let you take the plug out by pulling on a lever near the taps. You can spend ages playing with it.

But what exactly is a bidet for? And at what moment in the day is it used?

Having established that all my colleagues had a bidet in their respective bathrooms, I once enquired '*Alors, qu'est-ce que vous en faites?*' – so, what do you do with it? They promptly got extremely animated and all started talking at once. Seeing as I couldn't make any sense of what they were saying, I interrupted forcefully by stating that in our bathroom I used the bidet as a handy place to put the clean clothes that I was going to put on after my bath or shower so as to keep them dry and out of the way. Alternatively, I suggested, the bidet could be useful for dumping your dirty clothes prior to putting them in the washing machine. Enthused by the subject, I went on to explain that my wife has a different use for it: she enjoys reading in the bath but is never quite sure in advance which book or books she is going to want to read once she is in the water. Thus, for her, the bidet serves as a short-term bookcase for the great pile of books that she might find she wants to look at.

My colleagues, however, had other uses.

One, whose bathroom is very probably as chaotic as her office, explained how her bidet was used for storing make-up and cosmetics. This conjured up disturbing visions of a whole range of dusty tubes and pots of creams, half of which wouldn't have their tops screwed shut properly, dribbling their contents everywhere. Another, who had small children, had a more practical use: his bidet made a useful place for keeping his offspring's bath toys when they weren't being used.

The final colleague to express an opinion looked rather pleased with himself. He claimed that if you are having an amorous moment in the bath with someone, the bidet can make a handy ice bucket for the bottle of champagne. This comment so stunned us that conversation on the subject stopped completely.

Thus, no one seems quite sure what they are really for. Even less why they have taps on. Nevertheless, they do seem to feature strongly in a French day.

Incidentally, *un bidet* is also a French term for a pony. However, there is little scope for confusion as you don't often find ponies in bathrooms, even in France.

2. Faire la bise — a guide to shaking and kissing

Where I used to work in England, shaking hands was something generally allowed between two men, and very occasionally between a man and a woman, when they met for the very first time. When you were introduced to a new colleague you would shake hands politely and there it would end. The only possibility of shaking hands with anyone a second time would be if you were invited to their retirement party. If you stayed to the very end, when the final goodbyes were being exchanged, you were occasionally granted a second, clumsy handshake. Other than that, between introduction and retirement, no handshakes were expected at work unless you found yourself in a state of affectionate inebriation at a colleague's wedding. On such occasions, a congratulatory handshake with the groom could possibly be envisaged. This was something that only happened to me once in three years.

Outside work, shaking hands was equally rare. Kissing on cheeks, apart from with family or extremely close friends, was almost unheard of at the time. Thinking back, the most surprising thing is that I thought it quite normal in any kind of social situation to walk into a room full of people and make no greeting beyond a vague, collective 'Hi'.

This sort of behaviour would not go down well in France where handshaking and cheek-kissing are an essential part of daily life.

LA BISE

Faire la bise refers to the act of kissing someone on both cheeks, generally twice but sometimes four times and, more rarely, three times.

The term 'kiss on the cheeks' is deceptive because it is exactly what you don't do: two people can't kiss each other on the cheeks at the same time without dislocating their jaws. You have to put your cheeks side by side in brief contact and make a kissing sound out of the opposite side of your mouth. When changing from one side to the other, you have to keep your distance or you will bump noses. If you can, it is a good idea to practise on a close acquaintance before having a go on a real French person who knows how it should be done.

It is usually fairly easy to decide who to do *la bise* to: in a typical social encounter the men will do la bise to the women while the women will do it to everyone within reach whether man, woman or child. At longer social events there will be kissing of cheeks on arrival and on departure as there is with hand-shaking. But there may be times when you can't decide whether a bise is required in a given set of circumstances. It's all a matter of how well you know the person you are greeting, or even of how well you think you are going to end up knowing them.

Deux, trois ou quatre? Ou même six??

The number of kisses is another source of problems. Are you going to be relatively conventional and do two kisses, are you perhaps going to make it last as long as possible by doing four, or are you going to try to stand out from the crowd by doing three? You could possibly even opt for imitating people in deepest Brittany who, I am told, do six. If you opt for doing three or four, you are going to have to make this clear to the other person before, or possibly during, la bise. You do this by saying, '*Moi, c'est quatre* (or "*trois*")' as you start leaning towards the person in search of their cheek. They then have to take note of this right away so as to reconfigure their kissing strategy to avoid one of you stopping kissing before the other. Stopping mid-kiss is always awkward because one person starts pulling away while the other is still enthusiastically leaning forward for another bise. As soon as they realize this, both participants will hastily overreact to correct things. This invariably leads to bumping noses or even worse.

Interestingly enough, no one anywhere in France seems to do just one kiss on the cheek as a greeting.

À gauche ou à droite?

Even if you have fixed the number of kisses you are going to do, there is one final hurdle to overcome: which cheek do you start with? Everyone I know in the Paris area seems to start by tilting their head to the right. This brings both parties' left cheeks into contact with each other. But it seems that not everyone does this. I recently spent some time in Grenoble and was astonished to discover that everyone seemed to start off in the other direction, tilting the head to the left. This is extremely disconcerting as, if you lean the Parisian way, you find yourself with your head on one side, nose to nose with a very surprised-looking Grenobloise.

As soon as you realize that something is amiss, you instantly swing your head the other way ready to start again. Unfortunately, you are then faced with the same, still surprised Grenobloise who has just reacted in the same way as you. The only thing to do then is to pull back, smile somewhat uncomfortably and try to establish a mutually acceptable strategy.

Et au bureau?

One could imagine that once you get to work, you are safe from all this cheek-kissing. Sadly not. In all of the offices I have worked in, all the secretaries and assistants did la bise to each other every morning. Male assistants or colleagues of equal standing as the secretaries, regardless of age, were treated as honorary women and kissed accordingly. Also, young women, whatever their position in the department, tended to do la bise to other young women whether a social gap exists between them or not.

The idea of seeing a woman wander around an open-plan office first thing in the morning kissing cheeks all the while may well strike British office residents as odd. I once described the morning routine at work to an English friend and she exclaimed, 'Do you mean that when two women meet at work in the morning, they ask each other, "Have we snogged yet?"' In France no one even gives it a thought because, after all, it is just a form of greeting.

Et les enfants?

Given that you have decided to do la bise to a group of people, your problems aren't necessarily over. As we have seen, it is easier for women: they do la bise to anyone, whether other women, men or children. It is much more difficult for men. They are faced with a particular and tricky problem, namely that of greeting children. This is a procedure that is fraught with uncertainties. The best thing seems to be to leave it up to the child to decide if he or she wants to do la bise to you.

Thus, despite one or two difficulties, social kissing of cheeks is fairly easy to master. If you are in any doubt you can just leave it to whomever it is that you might be expected to kiss and follow their lead.

French kissing?

So, do they?

Do the French 'French kiss'?

Well, whatever they do, they don't call it *embrasser à la française*. And, disappointingly, they don't have a direct translation along the lines of *embrasser à l'anglaise*.

The basic word for 'to kiss' – *embrasser* – can cover both sorts of kissing, from affectionate on the cheek to full-on. However, the circumstances in which the word is used always make it easy to guess which sense is being talked about.

While they don't say *embrasser à la française*, they do have a couple of fitting expressions for having a good snog with someone, the sort of activity in which tongues feature at some point. These are *rouler une pelle* which literally means 'to roll a shovel' (perhaps French tongues are bigger than British ones?) and *rouler un patin* where *un patin* is 'a skate' or 'a pad'.

And so to the shaking of hands . . .

SERRER LA MAIN À QUELQU'UN

'To shake hands with someone' in French is *serrer la main à quelqu'un*. The English verb 'shake' refers to the slight up and down movement that you traditionally make with your hand when shaking hands with someone and formally saying, 'How do you do?' When French people shake hands there is none of this up and down movement, you just grasp the other person's hand and keep your hand immobile during the grasping process. This is reflected in the French word *serrer*, which means 'to grasp' and not 'to shake'.

The French are much amused by the British notion of shaking people's hands rather than just grasping them. This is brilliantly reflected in *Astérix chez les Bretons* where Astérix and Obelix go off and discover all that is odd on the other side of the Channel. In the French original text, the British characters speak French but use English expressions translated directly into French such as *bonté gracieuse* for 'good gracious'. These French expressions, being literal translations, don't actually mean anything at all. Thus, when the character Jolitorax offers to shake hands with Astérix and Obelix he says, '*Secouons-nous les mains!*' instead of the proper French expression, *Serrons-nous les mains*. For French readers this conjures up images of the participants violently shaking their hands as though to get the dust off them. As I am known to be English, '*Secouons-nous les mains*' is something that gets said surprisingly often when people greet me.

Entre amis

The basic rule of handshaking in France is simple: whenever a man meets a male friend or acquaintance for the first time in a given day, they will shake hands. Thus for example, if friends come to supper, I will shake hands with the men when they arrive. But I will also have to shake their hands again when they leave. The longer the visit lasts, the more handshaking there will be. If your friends stay overnight, they will probably expect to shake your hand when they head off to bed last thing. But, in the morning, when they stumble down to breakfast, you might think that, having spent the night in your house and shaken hands at least twice the day before, there would be no need to start the day with yet another shake. Far from it. The night has wiped the handshaking slate clean and you will have to start shaking hands all over again before your guests can even think about pouring themselves a cup of coffee.

Even the people that you see regularly will expect a handshake each and every time you see them. I regularly bump into our next-door neighbour outside our house, either at weekends or in the morning when I'm on my way to the station and he is out walking his dog. Each time, however brief the conversation, there will be a preliminary handshake. But this doesn't only apply to friends and acquaintances. I will be expected to shake hands with our postman before I have any chance of being given the day's post. And any kind of remotely professional encounter, whether at the dentist, hairdresser or at a restaurant where they recognize us, will be marked by handshakes at the beginning and at the end. There is even a good chance that the man who delivers our heating oil, or the bloke from the water company who comes to read the meter, will offer a hand to be shaken at least once during his visit.

Au bureau

My French male colleagues revealed themselves to be inveterate handshakers from my very first day at the office. However, as nothing is ever simple, there appear to be two schools of thought about when all this handshaking should actually take place. The more outgoing seem to feel that it is terribly important to go round the entire office of some thirty people to greet everyone as soon as they get to work each morning. Some even set off on their rounds the minute they have hung up their coat. While hands are shaken, the actual exchange never extends much beyond a brief '*Bonjour. Ça va?*' The reply is hardly more scintillating, being generally limited to something along the lines of '*Salut. Ça va, et toi?*' as the instigator of the greeting is already drifting towards the door on his way to greet someone else.

The alternative strategy – which I have adopted – is the greet-people-as-you-meet-them one. This has the advantage of preventing you from having to spend half an hour wandering from office to office shaking hands with people. You are then free to spend that half hour doing something useful like reading the paper.

'*On s'est vu ce matin?*'

There is one main disadvantage of the greet-people-as-you-meet-them strategy: you have to remember whom you have already met in a given day. If you get it wrong and try to shake hands with someone whom you have already seen that day, they won't actually get cross but they may well make some mildly critical comment about your apparently having been half asleep the first time you met. They may even try to suggest various dubious things that you have been thinking about to make you forget them so readily.

Of course, the larger the number of colleagues you have, the harder it is to remember exactly which ones you have greeted. Even with a few colleagues you can still bump into someone at any time from about mid-morning onwards and realize that neither of you can decide whether you have already greeted each other or not that day. Both of you stop and look at each other fixedly, a puzzled expression on each face, before one, or possibly both, tentatively, and slowly, extends a hand while frowning doubtfully. Once your hands are almost touching, you will be struck by the idea that it would perhaps be wise to check whether a handshake is, in fact, really called for. You will say something like, '*On s'est vu ce matin?*' – have we seen each other this morning? – in an interrogative tone. This relieves you completely of all the burden of deciding whether you have already shaken hands that day. If the other person decides that you haven't already greeted each other that day, you will carry on and complete the handshake, making some trivial remark about becoming forgetful or growing old. Conversely, if your colleague clearly remembers shaking your hand and can assure you of the time and location of the incident, you pull back your hand, smiling apologetically before continuing on your way.

Les groupes

The problem with all this handshaking is that it can be really very time-consuming. If I am in a group walking down a corridor and we meet another group, and at least one of them knows at least one of us, we all have to stop and shake hands with everyone in the other group. Such group-encounter handshaking serves no real purpose: the only valuable handshakes are the ones between the people who actually know each other. The remaining hand-shaking is just done out of politeness to avoid any of the others feeling left out.

Just occasionally, in one of these group-handshaking encoun-ters, some people will try to justify the whole operation by mumbling their names as they stretch out their hands. If they imagine that they are doing it for my benefit, they are mistaken because I am incapable of remembering five or six ordinary English surnames when mumbled rapidly one after the other, let alone six strange French ones. Name mumbling is a good example of how cruelly I was duped by my French O-level. The lessons lulled me into believing that everyone in France is called something simple like Dupont or Martin or, in exceptional cases, Bardot or Deneuve. Such names are common enough, though I can't say I have ever met a Bardot, even less a Deneuve. Unfortunately, I seem to keep meeting people with astonishing regional names like Burguburu or L'Helgouach which are completely impossible to understand, let alone remember, when mumbled hurriedly to me in a corridor.

The only people who won't shake your hand are those who are sulking. A previous boss was a prolific sulker. His sulking was notable for both the low level of offence that could set it off, and the time a sulk could last once it had been provoked. I used to upset him a lot, even occasionally by accident, and each time he would sulk for a couple of days. It was easy to spot a sulk because when I failed to avoid him in the corridor and stretched out a hypocritical hand, he would turn his head away sharply and march on past.

3. Je t'aime –
the romantic side of things

The French would have us believe that theirs is the language of love and they may well be right. Whether the language is particularly suited for love or not, the French version of the rhyme that you recite when you want flower petals to tell you how your love life is going has a lot to be said for it.

In the English version, you take a flower and pull off the petals one by one saying alternately, 'She [or he] loves me; she loves me not . . .'

The French version is far more comprehensive:

> *Elle m'aime* [or, of course, *il m'aime*]:
> *Un peu,*
> *Beaucoup,*
> *Passionnément,*
> *À la folie,*
> *Pas du tout.*

This not only tells you whether you are loved or not, it gives you an idea of how much you are loved, assuming you are, ranging from a little, to a lot, to passionately, to wildly. It also gives you a much better chance of the news being good. In the English version, you have a 50 per cent chance of unhappiness: she doesn't love you as often as she does. In France the chances of being loved are 80 per cent, with only a 20 per cent chance that you aren't.

Clearly, if you want to have the best chance of good news, you should question the flower in French.

DRAGUER

Before you get to the happy stage where you can ask flowers about the prospects for your love life, you first have to meet a suitable person.

It being many long years since I last tried to chat anyone up (in English or in French), I thought I would ask the various adolescents who frequent our house what chat-up lines they favour. Their replies were so diverse, complicated and, in several cases, alarmingly unsubtle, that I thought that it would be best to stick to something traditional. In the UK, classic chat-up lines are supposed to include such sure-fire winners as 'Do you come here often?' and, though I am sure no living person has ever said it, 'Would you like to come up and see my etchings?'

If you want to *draguer* – flirt – in France there are two classic lines to choose from. The first is *'Est-ce que vous habitez chez vos parents?'* – do you live with your parents? – though I don't see what you do with the information once you know whether they do or not. Nevertheless, there are many people who attribute their married bliss to their use of this line.

The second line corresponds closely to the British etchings question, though the artwork in question is slightly more exotic. It is *'Voulez-vous venir voir mes estampes japonaises?'* – would you like to see my Japanese engravings? I don't know about you, but I am incapable of identifying a Japanese engraving, even with the light on. Even less an etching. I am assured by various French people who don't know what *estampes* are either that it doesn't matter because once she or he has agreed to come up and see them, it is a fairly simple matter to deftly change the subject and gloss over the fact that your room contains no Japanese artworks of any description.

Another possibility, though probably not for the younger generation, is to use Jean Gabin's immortal line to Michèle Morgan in the 1938 film, *Quai des brumes*. He says to her, '*T'as de beaux yeux, tu sais*' – you've got beautiful eyes, you know. If the girl knows her films, you could strike lucky because Michèle Morgan replies, '*Embrasse-moi!*' – kiss me!

'ET PLUS, SI AFFINITÉS'

If the preceding quick guide to French chat-up lines has, inexplicably, failed to bring success, and you are still seeking a partner, you might resort to reading the personal adverts in a French paper. The structure and form of these are essentially the same as in the UK, with abbreviations being used extensively. Thus, a young man (Jeune Homme) seeking a young woman (Jeune Femme) will start his advert with 'JH cherche JF' before going on to describe his qualities and those of the JF he is seeking. The key phrase, one that has entered day-to-day vocabulary, comes at the end of the advert. The JH will explain that he wants to meet the JF for friendship, walks in the country, going to the cinema and other such innocent pastimes. But he will, of course, be hoping for something a bit more exciting and will therefore want to try to keep his options open. Thus, he will end his advert with the phrase, '... *et plus, si affinités*'. This means, roughly, '... and more, if we get on OK'. Everyone knows what the *plus* actually means. The phrase has become so well known that some of my colleagues use it in emails as a joke when organizing meetings. At least, I assume it is a joke.

LE MARIAGE

With a bit of luck, all the contact ads combined with a good bit of flirting may lead to a happy outcome.

The unusual thing about a French church wedding is that it has no legal value. If you get married in a church, whether Catholic or Protestant, you also have to have a civil ceremony in order to be considered as properly married in the eyes of the law. This is hard to grasp because, at first glance, a church wedding seems to contain all the essential ingredients of a marriage service. Surely the principal tenets of marriage are religious in origin? This is not so in French eyes. It all seems to stem from the fact that, whereas in England the Queen is both head of state and head of the Anglican Church, in France the head of state has no religious role at all.

There is nothing in France which corresponds to an English registry office because all civil weddings are carried out at the *mairie* – town hall – of the town or village where you live. Every community will have its mairie headed by its elected *maire* – mayor – who officiates at civil weddings. You can of course just get married before the maire and forego a church ceremony. The reverse is not possible. The presence of two separate elements of the wedding ceremony, church and mayor, makes a French wedding, and the invitations to attend, somewhat more complex than in Britain. Couples who decide to get married in church generally have the civil ceremony beforehand. Some people choose to have the civil ceremony in the morning and the church service in the afternoon of the same day. Other couples have the two parts on different days, sometimes weeks apart. Generally, only close family attend the civil service while all the guests attend the church ceremony. However, if the two are on the same day, everyone can be invited to both. Invitations have to be sent for each of the two occasions and have to make quite clear which one the guest is invited to. Guests can also just be invited to *le vin d'honneur* – a drinks party – which is held after the ceremony at *la mairie*. In this case, you generally need a separate invitation if there is a meal afterwards. Inviting someone only to the *vin d'honneur* is a good way of involving them in your wedding without having to spend a fortune.

The really good thing about French weddings is that you are expected to do some extravagant hooting on your way from the church to the reception. Wherever you happen to be in France on a Saturday, you may find your afternoon enlivened by a passing cavalcade of wildly hooting, be-ribboned cars. There is no particular rhythm to follow: it is just a happy random series of hoots. People coming the other way are expected to join in too. Unfortunately, our wedding was a bit of a disappointment in this respect. While I had gone to the trouble of adding some extra-powerful air horns to our car for the occasion, and used them to good effect on the road back from *la mairie*, few other cars hooted. The English contingent didn't hoot because I had forgotten to tell them about the French tradition, while my new family-in-law didn't hoot because, incurable snobs that they are, they think hooting is common.

La belle famille

In France the concept of *la belle famille* – in-laws – is broader than that in the UK where the term brother-in-law is limited to my wife's brother or my sister's husband. Seen from a French point of view, my *beau-frère* – brother-in-law – also includes my wife's sister's husband, while my wife's brother's wife is my *belle-sœur* – sister-in-law. Having more brothers- and sisters-in-law than you would otherwise have may well strike you as a great reason to come to live in France. But why do they use the words *beau* or *belle*? Are French familys-in-law more beautiful or handsome than anyone else's? Apparently not: it seems that the use of these words goes back to the Middle Ages where they were originally used simply as a mark of affection. French brothers- and sisters-in-law thus may be more numerous than in the UK but they are not necessarily any better looking. Unless, of course, they're mine.

LA MAÎTRESSE – ALTERNATIVE LUNCHTIME ACTIVITIES AT WORK

You may be happy in the belief that the allure of their *entrée, plat et dessert* is so strong that all French people spend their lunchtimes at work eating at the canteen.

Unfortunately, this is not necessarily the case.

Surprising as it may seem, some French people, notably in my experience those who work in the offices of large companies, are prepared to forego their meals in favour of other activities of a, not to put too fine a point on it, physical nature.

Rather than make sweeping generalizations (which is not

something I would ever do), I am going to give two examples of what people got up to in the offices of my previous employer. Sadly, no one seems to do that kind of thing where I now work. It must be something that they put in the tea ...

A colleague in my old department, a chap who, despite having reached fifty, was considered by many to be *bien conservé* – better than average for his age – only had lunch with the rest of us on very special occasions. On the majority of other days he had his own particular lunchtime routine. This was always the same. (I know this because his office was opposite mine.) At 11.45 he would ring an internal number and say, '*Oui, c'est moi ... On y va?*' – it's me ... shall we go? The conversation never varied from day to day except on the rare occasions when the person's phone was answered by a colleague. This was always obvious because instead of the usual, '*Oui, c'est moi ...*', there was a moment of stammering confusion followed by a request for whoever it was to leave a message to ring his extension number. He never, ever left his name. Once she had rung back (for it is only fair to make clear that it was a she) and the '*On y va?*' had met with a favourable response, my colleague, Claude, set off down the corridor to the lifts, whistling cheerfully. It was widely known that Claude rented a small flat in one of the few residential towers that were built among the office buildings and that he and the unnamed lady (whom everyone knew by sight) were headed there.

At two o'clock on the dot, Claude would return to his office. The whole department knew that if he returned whistling a cheery tune, his lunchtime mission had been accomplished successfully. This was so well known in the office that a brief and cheery bit of whistling was used in office conversation as a euphemism for sex.

Surprisingly enough, no one gossiped about Claude: it was just an accepted fact of our office life. It was, however, vital never, ever to whistle in the corridor when returning from your own lunch because that really would have been a cause for gossip.

Claude and the unnamed lady were among the lucky ones because they had a nice, warm flat, apparently with a wonderful view of our building, to go to at lunchtimes. Others were not so fortunate. They had to make do with what they could get when they set out to avoid eating lunch.

One of our department's secretaries, who came to work by car and who parked in the underground car park below our tower, went out to do some shopping one lunchtime. Sometime later, she was seen staggering back into the office with a number of carrier bags. When asked why she hadn't left them in her car, she blushed and explained that she hadn't been able to get to it. It turned out that when she had gone down to the car park with her shopping, she had been faced with the car parked right next to hers rebounding softly on its springs. Moving closer to find out the cause she was faced with a lightly clad couple in the midst of what she described as moderately pleasurable activity. She apparently based this conclusion on seeing the bored expression on the face of the woman in the car, whom, incidentally, she had easily recognized as being someone from the floor below ours.

She didn't need to try to recognize the car, even less the man's bottom, because its owner's name was neatly printed on a plaque on the car-park wall.

LE PORNO

Several people have encouraged me to finish this chapter with something a bit X certificate. It isn't really that sort of book, but I thought I would give it a go.

Les films classés X

French pornographic film titles are often more amusing than the films in question (or so I have been told). This is apparently because there are people whose job it is to spend their day making up suitable titles for X-rated films. The attraction of such jobs is more limited than first appears as they don't actually get to see any of the films whose titles they are creating. Someone else, who has presumably seen the film, has the job of putting the title and the film together.

For example, the French version of *Snow White and the Seven Dwarfs* is *Blanche-Neige et les Sept Nains*. Some bright spark was inspired by this to come up with the pornographic film title *Blanches fesses et les sept mains* – White buttocks and the seven hands.

Everyone seems to know the title though no one admits to actually having seen the film.

Les livres cochons

One of the principal uses of X-rated literature is as a good test of how well you have mastered a language. If you imagine that you are sitting beside someone who is reading an English book and you happen to glance at the page they are reading, you will instantly spot any 'rude' bits. Your brain, all by itself, somehow manages to focus on the 'rude' words, which seem to stand out from all the other words on the page. Please tell me that it isn't just me. In my experience, it's a very long time indeed before you can do that in a foreign language. For a start, there is a whole special vocabulary to learn. Then, even when you have learnt the words in question, you have to have reached a high level of familiarity with all the other day-to-day words before you can start to spot the rude from the ordinary.

This is all becoming a bit too revealing so let's move on rapidly to an example of *un livre cochon* – a pornographic book – title.

The Harry Potter books are all the rage in France where they have titles like *Harry Potter et la Coupe de Feu*. The books refer to Harry and his magic wand as *Harry Potter et sa baguette magique*. This inspired an 'adult' book which I spotted the other day at our local FNAC (the adult books are inexplicably just next to the books in English) called *Harry Peloteur et la braguette magique*. This is doubly amusing: *un peloteur* is 'a groper' and *braguette magique* means 'magic flies' – in the trouser-zip sense.

4. Tu ou vous? – is it thou or you?

No one says 'thou' any more, except, of course, to God. This is something for which the British should perhaps be more grateful.

Speaking to people in English, now that 'thou' is no longer used, is a lot easier than many foreign language speakers believe because there is only one word to express the concept of 'you'. Regardless of how well you know somebody, whether you are talking to a complete stranger or your twin brother, it makes no difference to the word you use. You can shriek insults, address royalty, flirt outrageously or just ask someone the time, but the word you use will always be the same: 'you'.

People in France are not so lucky. They have to make an important decision each time they address anyone. This is because there are two words for 'you' in French: *tu* and *vous*.

Tu is for people you know well while *vous* is for people you don't know and also for addressing more than one person collectively, whether you know them or not.

It seems simple enough at first sight: you say *tu* to friends, family, small children and domestic animals; you say *vous* to everyone else – in other words, anyone you don't know well enough to say *tu* to. And also to groups of people.

Thus, when you come to France on holiday you should expect to say *vous* to everyone you speak to, with the possible exception of any friends, family, small children and domestic animals that you may find yourself chatting to.

Unfortunately, because French verbs conjugate (something that English ones don't do as much) the verb that you are using won't be the same if you say *tu* as it is if you say *vous*. For example, if you take *aimer* – to love – the phrase 'you love' is *tu aimes* or *vous aimez* depending on which word for 'you' you pick.

This comes to light as soon as you start to make sentences in French. What's more, not only are they different, but verb forms when using *vous* are usually much more complicated to construct and, above all, harder to pronounce, than when using *tu*. Verbs with *vous* seem always to have an extra vowel stuck in at exactly the place where it is hardest to pronounce. Something simple like 'you wanted' is quite easy using the *tu* form – *tu voulais* – but in the *vous* form the verb gets an extra 'i' and makes you struggle to pronounce all the vowels properly – *vous vouliez*. It doesn't seem much when it is written down like that but somehow, in practice, it makes all the difference between a sentence which you pronounce almost fluently and one that causes you to stumble and hesitate.

This is bad news for English people who have to use *vous* forms when on holiday.

'TU' NOT 'VOUS'

When I first came to France on holiday to stay with my future parents-in-law, I should have been expected to say *tu* to my future brothers- and sisters-in-law while saying *vous* to all family members older than me. I struggled bravely for the whole of the first day, trying my best with the common verbs that seem to crop up in polite conversation such as *voudriez-vous* . . . – would you like . . . – with its annoying middle 'i'. Then, on the second day, realism coupled with a fair bit of natural laziness forced me to act. 'Stuff this!' I thought. 'If I'm going to be able to communicate at all, I'm going to have to make things as easy for myself as possible: it will have to be *tu* for everyone.' From that day on, I unilaterally declared that I should use the *tu* form with all members of Inès's family, whether brothers, sisters, parents or even grandmother. To say that this strategy created a stir would be an understatement.

Despite causing some raised eyebrows, I got away with it because the people in question knew who I was. It would not have worked at all with strangers such as shopkeepers, barmen or policemen. If you try saying *tu* to anyone like that, they will most likely react quite angrily. Especially policemen.

'VOUS' TO 'TU'

So, when you meet anyone in France you will be expected to address them as *vous*. Once you get to know them better, you will be allowed to think about changing over to *tu*.

Changing from the formal to the familiar is a process that is fraught with difficulties. For a start, once you have made the change, you can never go back. When two people change from a formal to a friendly, familiar level of conversation, they are stuck with it. Even if they have a blazing row, or try to stab each other, they cannot go back to saying *vous*.

This means that even French people tend to think carefully about things before making the leap to familiarity.

If two people have been talking to each other for some time, they may reach a point in their relationship where they both feel that they can move to a friendlier level and start to *tutoyer* – use *tu* with each other. The progression from *vous* to *tu* can take anything from five minutes to several months. This will make both parties feel that they have become closer. At an appropriate moment, one person will say to the other something like, '*On peut se dire "tu" maintenant?*' – we can say *tu* to each other now? – and, if the situation has been judged correctly, the other will agree and the friendship will blossom.

Some people take it upon themselves to act unilaterally and switch to saying *tu* without consulting the other party. One moment they are saying *vous* and suddenly the next sentence is full of *tu*s. For the other person this can be good news or bad: if they have been thinking of changing over too, they will take the opportunity of doing so without anything more being said. On the other hand, if they feel that the relationship hasn't reached such a height of intimacy, they may be somewhat displeased. They might grumble a bit, saying something like, 'Oh, I see we are going to say *tu* now', and duly change over, or they might resolutely carry on saying *vous* to show that they are not pleased at all about this unwelcome familiarity. This is generally the end of a budding friendship.

Once you start saying *tu* to certain people, you will find that your memory has to improve. With any given person, you will have to remember their name, whether you like them, whether you kiss them on the cheeks (and if so, how often) or whether you shake their hand, and whether you address them as *tu* or *vous*. This requires quite a sophisticated mental filing system.

'VOUS' NOT 'TU'

When it comes to families talking among themselves, you could be forgiven for assuming that everyone calls each other *tu*, whether it's parents talking to their children or the children replying; and, of course, practically everyone does. But there is, increasingly rarely, the occasional old-fashioned family where the parents insist on their children addressing them as *vous*. This is either because the poor parents are living in the past or because they are trying to give an impression of pseudo-nobility. Children of such families, which frequently seem to feature retired colonels somewhere in their ranks, tend not only to say *vous* to their parents, but also to call them *Mère et Père* instead of the more usual *Maman et Papa*. This is the equivalent of calling your mum and dad 'Mother and Father'. I have even come across one really peculiar family where the only child was allowed to call her father *tu* but had to address her mother as *vous*.

'VOUS' *AND* 'TU'

In some social situations you can find yourself in the same room as some people calling each other *vous* and others calling each other *tu*. This can happen, for example, if you invite two sets of friends to supper at your house. All the people that you have invited are your friends – you wouldn't have invited them otherwise – so, obviously, you call them all *tu*. But they haven't met each other before and will thus have to address each other as *vous* while of course still saying *tu* to you. This sort of thing doesn't matter much if it only lasts a few minutes, but if no one does anything you are going to find yourself in an uncomfortable group of people, some of whom are being formal with each other, while others are being more relaxed and friendly. You will be sitting there, happily cracking jokes and making stupid comments to each set of friends while they will be saying *vous* to each other and, by definition, being much more formal and dull. Of course, there is nothing to stop you making jokes while saying *vous*; they just won't seem as funny as they would using *tu*.

If there is going to be any chance of saving your evening and stopping the conversation from becoming stilted, one set of friends has to take the initiative and suggest using *tu* to the others. You should thus try to take care when picking your guests so as to ensure that they are likely to get on and to want to *tutoyer*. Clearly, if they don't like the look of each other they are not going to be keen on becoming too familiar. As a last resort, if your friends seem to be getting on, but are so hopeless that none of them has dared suggest that they all use *tu*, you can try and impose it upon them. You are fairly sure of succeeding if you do because if either lot refused they would look incredibly churlish.

'TU ...!'

Given that you are supposed to *vouvoyer* – use *vous* – with strangers you can actually use *tu* as a sort of weapon to show how angry you are about something. If you have an argument with someone you don't know – someone who has cut you up on the road or pushed in front of you in a queue, for example – you can add extra insult to whatever offensive thing you are saying by using the *tu* form. I was on a bus in Paris which got cut up by a van. A few hundred metres further on, the bus driver threw his bus in front of the van, causing it to screech to a halt, opened his door and yelled out, *'Tu me diras si je te gêne!'* – let me know if I'm in your way at all! It was the use of *tu* that made this such a splendid put-down and got him a round of applause from all the passengers.

Of course, this sort of thing is extremely risky for a foreign visitor to do.

'TU' AND 'VOUS' AT WORK

In the workplace, it is also tricky deciding which form of address to use.

The average person at work is likely to have some colleagues below them in the pecking order, some at the same level and, probably, a whole lot more above. When you first join a company you will say *vous* to everyone. Assuming that you are able to tell those below you what to do, you will generally continue to say *vous* to them because saying *tu* to someone to whom you give instructions often causes problems in the 'familiarity breeds contempt' way of things.

Similarly, you will also carry on saying *vous* to those above you for the same reasons because being seen to be on familiar terms with your boss is not necessarily a good thing either.

Thus, you will say *tu* only to colleagues who are your equals and to those you like.

NEITHER 'TU' NOR 'VOUS'

An engineering student once came to our office for three months' work experience. Jean-Philippe proved astonishingly pleasant and was especially knowledgeable about Six Nations Rugby, and so very quickly I switched to saying *tu* to him. I invited him to say *tu* to me, of course, as I had to do, being much older, but he carried on politely calling me *vous*. I assumed that he would settle down after a few days and drop the formality, but the *vouvoiement* carried on and on. It wasn't that we didn't get on, it was rather that Jean-Philippe felt that, as he was the student and I was the 'master', I deserved a bit of respect. After a few weeks of me saying *tu* and Jean-Philippe replying with *vous* we set off on a business trip together. In the plane, faced with yet another use of *vous*, I asked Jean-Philippe quite sharply to stop messing about with *vouvoiement* and to get on and call me *tu*. Clearly much embarrassed, he promised faithfully that he would do so. At supper that night, I noticed that all Jean-Philippe's remarks were constructed in the most tortuous and convoluted fashion: '*Pourrait-on . . .*' or '*Ne serait-il pas possible de . . .*' – might one . . . or would it not be possible for . . . – or any number of sentences containing the word *on* – one. I couldn't work out what he was playing at. His questions finished with '*n'est-ce pas?*' – isn't it? – where he should have been expected to say, 'don't you think?' It took ages for me to realize what he was up to: there was not a single *vous* or *tu* anywhere to be seen. It was masterful. I spent a whole evening chatting most convivially with a person who wouldn't say 'you' to me at all.

IL/ELLE

There is one alternative to using *tu* or *vous* which you will probably only ever hear used in shops. If the salesperson can't decide whether to call you *tu* or *vous*, or can't be bothered to call you either, they might call you *il* or *elle*. It may even be intended as a peculiar form of politeness. When it comes to your turn to be served, they will turn to you and enquire, '*Qu'est-ce qu'il veut?*' or, of course, '*Qu'est-ce qu'elle veut?*' – what does he/she want? In some cases they may say, '*Qu'est-ce que je lui sers?*' – what shall I serve him/her? It can be very disconcerting to be addressed as though you weren't really there, or to be given the impression that the salesperson is actually talking to someone invisible. The first time it happened to me I actually turned round to see who the girl was talking to.

The only other people who seem to use *il* or *elle* as a way of saying 'you' are nurses who deal with elderly patients. I have it on good authority that elderly patients are often spoken to in the third person. *Il* or *elle* is also used as an admonishment. A nurse might complain that a patient hasn't taken their pills by grumbling, '*Elle n'a pas pris ses médicaments.*'

5. Oh, la, la! – how to gesticulate and exclaim

It should really come as no surprise that it was France, rather than any other country, that produced the famous Marcel Marceau.

For a typical French person is able to convey a huge range of feelings and emotions without actually having to say a word. Hands, arms, face and even occasionally the entire upper body can be called upon either to take the place of a spoken word or, more often, to illustrate and add weight to something important that is being said. French people are born to gesticulate: they can do it without any conscious thought. I am convinced that they can even do it in their sleep.

All this has resulted in a great range of French gestures, far more than are seen in Britain.

If you are prepared to concentrate and use a bit of imagination, and hopefully act them out, even if you are reading this on public transport, I'm sure you'll be able to master the following examples.

HAUSSER LES ÉPAULES

We shall start with the most fundamental of all French gestures: the classic Gallic shrug.

Were shrugging an Olympic sport, the French would be sure of winning the gold medal every four years. The French shrug often, and they shrug splendidly. 'To shrug' in French is *hausser les épaules*, a term that you will not hear often, but you will see the act in question countless times.

Anyone can shrug: faced with a problem or a situation that

59

leaves you indifferent or uncertain, you just raise both shoulders rapidly, before letting them fall back to their usual positions. This is a basic shrug which lets everyone know that you don't really care much about whatever it is you are actually shrugging about.

While it conveys this basic meaning perfectly satisfactorily, such a perfunctory shrug won't get you far in France. In France, when you shrug, your whole upper body has to be involved, especially your arms and hands. Indeed, there are those for whom the full essence of a shrug can only be conveyed by using almost every part of the body, including the hips and knees. However, we will not be dealing with such advanced shrugging here. It is too complex a subject to be explained without the use of extensive video footage.

So, please try to imagine that you have been confronted with some situation, be it in a bar, a shop or in front of a market stall, which leaves you generally indifferent but also somewhat uncertain as to how to continue. You are thinking something like, 'That's the way life is', or, possibly, 'Frankly my dear, I don't give a damn.' Or even, 'What the hell do you expect me to do in these circumstances?' But you don't want to convey this verbally, though you do want to convey it clearly. So, standing up, prepare to do four things simultaneously: raise both shoulders and hold them raised for at least two and a half seconds; while doing this, turn your head slightly to one side (it doesn't matter which); turn the sides of your mouth down for the same two-and-a-half-second period; and, most importantly, raise both forearms to a horizontal position, while turning the thumbs outwards so that both palms are in a horizontal plane. I have just reread this while standing in front of the computer and it works perfectly. My wife has just asked what the matter is.

A final little detail, once you have mastered the shrug, is to breathe out despondently while holding the position. It is the little thing that makes the whole gesture perfect.

OH, LA, LA!

Whenever I think of one of my first French work colleagues, Nicolas, this gesture comes to mind. It was something I hadn't really seen before starting work in France as no one in my family-in-law uses it. (Needless to say, they believe that the gesture is common.) I think of it as the *Oh, la, la* gesture and it is used by someone when they tell you something that they consider remarkable, unexpected or even astonishing, the sort of thing that provokes surprise, complicity or a cry of *Oh, la, la!* from their listener. As they reach the exciting bit in the story, they will shake the fingers of one hand rapidly as though they were wet and they wanted to shake off the drops of water. Purists will want to know that the hand is held in front of the body, level with the elbow, and that about four shaking movements are considered sufficient. Of course, when you have just said something astonishing, your face has a role to play too. Despite my term for the gesture, the person making it doesn't actually say *Oh, la, la* – or anything at all. The gesture replaces the words.

For example, if Nicolas described the model from Balmain with whom he had been lucky enough to share the lift that morning, he would say, '*Elle était vraiment bien*' – she was really pretty – or '*Elle était vraiment canon*' – she was astonishingly pretty – while enthusiastically shaking his fingers. The excellent wine he had drunk at a friend's house the night before would also be described with a shake and something like, '*Ah! Qu'est-ce qu'il était bon!*' – it was incredibly good. The gesture could be used for other purposes too. Nicolas once witnessed our boss giving a lowly colleague a terrible ticking off for some minor crime. When I asked for details he just opened his eyes very wide, whistled and shook his fingers animatedly. He didn't need to say anything: from the gesture alone I could guess exactly what had happened. Of course, Nicolas wasn't the only one to use the *Oh, la, la* gesture: what was special about his way of doing it was that he managed to make his fingers slap against each other as he shook his hand so his gesture actually made a snapping sound which no one else's seemed to do.

Next time you read an Astérix cartoon book, you will probably spot one of the characters making this gesture somewhere in the background.

'IL FAIT FROID' – THE COLD FINGERS GESTURE

If you want to show that you are cold in the UK, you will probably do an exaggerated form of shivering. You may even hug yourself while doing it to add a bit of emphasis. In France, when you want to convey how really very cold something is – the weather, for example – you do the cold fingers gesture. To do this, you group the tips of all your fingers and your thumb together in a bunch, bring them close to your mouth as though you were going to kiss them and then, before they actually touch your lips, blow sharply on them a couple of times while making appropriate, wide-eyed facial gestures of surprise. While blowing on your fingers, you have to open and close the bunch a couple of times too. Only then will the other person understand just how cold it is.

LE BRAS D'HONNEUR

Having dealt with some neutral, non-aggressive gestures, we could perhaps look at a less friendly one. A *bras d'honneur* is the non-verbal means of saying '— you!' or '— off!'

Please spread the book out wide and put it on the table in front of you while you stand up. Once you are standing up you are going to hit the inside of your right elbow with the palm of your left hand. You should therefore stretch out your right arm, palm uppermost, and then bring your left hand sharply across. As your left hand hits your right elbow, snap your right forearm up into the air. You have a choice to make at this point: either you can snap your forearm up with a clenched fist, or you can leave your fingers straight. It seems that the crosser you are, the tighter your fingers. Thus, if you are really displeased you make a fist, while if you are a bit more indifferent about whatever it is, you leave your fingers loose.

LA BARBE

I have said that the French have gestures for all sorts of things: they even have one for being bored. Something boring in French is *barbant*. An exclamation when bored is *la barbe!*, which means 'the beard'. Inexplicably, when faced with something tedious, a

French person is heard to exclaim, '*Oh! La barbe!*' to convey how little they feel like doing the thing in question.

Rather than actually talking about beards, you can mime one to show how fed up you are. However, you are not trying to mime a great big bushy beard of the sort sported by Arctic explorers; you just want to show that there is a bit of stubble. To do this, you rub the backs of your fingers along the side of your chin a couple of times, fairly rapidly. As with all these gestures, if you don't know what it means, it is very difficult to guess from someone apparently rubbing their chin that they are bored or fed up. Despite the fact that they generally don't have beards – at least not when they are younger – French women are allowed to make this gesture too.

'*MON ŒIL!*'

We have dealt with despondency, astonishment, cold, anger and boredom. We will now attempt a gesture that shows disbelief or scepticism.

There is an expression that is used to show that you don't entirely believe what someone has just said to you, namely, *Mon œil!* This means 'my eye' – also used as an expression in English.

Again, the French don't just have the expression; they have a gesture to go with it, or rather to go in place of it. Imagine you are listening to someone who is telling a story that strikes you as just too good to be true and you want to express your feelings on the matter. Rather than saying, '*Mon œil!*' in a sceptical tone, you just press your index fingertip to the skin just below your eye and pull it down a little bit while making your best sceptical expression. Whether the story is actually true or not, showing raw scepticism by making the *mon œil* gesture at someone will generally be seen as extremely annoying and even provocative. It's best to look out for this being done by someone else, but not to risk doing it yourself.

There are plenty more gestures we could look at but it is time to move on to something that is even tougher to explain.

'NON'

We have spent the last few minutes in a frenzy of arm-waving and gesturing. As a bit of light relief, we are now going to attempt a bit of non-verbal communication. The aim of this is to be able to say *Non* to a French person without actually pronouncing the word itself. (Please don't ask why we should want to do this; we just do.) It is quite easy: all you have to do is make a 'tut tut' sound with your tongue against the roof of your mouth, like a quieter, more refined version of someone trying to urge on a horse or a train of huskies. As it is a negative sound, you need to show indifference or even displeasure by keeping your face resolutely immobile. While your face doesn't move, you can add emphasis to the operation by wagging your index finger back and forth like a small metronome. This sort of finger-wagging can sometimes be a sign of *Non* all on its own. Finally, in cases of extreme agitation, you are allowed to make head-shaking movements, though they must be so slight as to be almost undetectable. Such head shaking is reserved for very serious situations such as, 'No, you cannot have an ice-cream!'

It is unlikely that anyone will 'tut tut' at you while you are on holiday. However, if you are very observant, you may well spot it being done to someone else. The finger-wagging is a good clue to look out for.

A FEW USEFUL EXPRESSIONS

Short, sharp expressions that suit a particular situation are as common in French as they are in English. The sort of English expressions I am thinking about are, 'Well done!'; 'See you'; 'Here!'; 'Not bad' . . . The problem with these sorts of expression is twofold: first of all, you have to learn them; secondly, you have to be sure that you use the correct one for the job. I can't bring myself to relate any of the numerous and all-too-painful examples of situations where I used entirely the wrong expression for the circumstances, so I shall take the easy way out by telling you about our friend Polly.

Bien fait!

Having studied the language over a fair number of years, Polly's command of French is quite impressive. Unfortunately, she had somehow come to assume that the English cry of 'Well done!' when faced with some impressive act should be literally translated as '*Bien fait!*' The only slight problem is that, while the words literally mean 'well done', the expression *Bien fait!* actually means 'serves you right'. The misunderstanding came to light on a visit to Paris. Polly was walking down a flight of steps in the Métro when a woman in front of her slipped and only narrowly avoided falling flat on her face by deftly catching the handrail at the last possible second. Wanting, in all innocence, to express her admiration for the woman's skill in saving herself, Polly cheerily cried, '*Bien fait!*' The woman, barely recovered from the indignities and discomfort of her close call, was faced with the confusing spectacle of a charming Englishwoman, smiling winningly, who was apparently delighting in her misfortune. It was only when Polly asked us to translate some of what the poor woman had yelled at her that she discovered the error of her ways.

Allez! Viens!

This has always struck me as the most contradictory of expressions as *aller* means 'to go' while *venir* means 'to come'. You can use the imperative of aller, *Allez!*, in all sorts of ways – from *Allez les Bleus* to encourage the French team, to a long, wheedling *Allleeeez* to try and get someone to do something they don't want to do. You can also punctuate a sharp instruction by adding a brisk *Allez!* at the end, meaning '. . . and get a move on!'

But when you want to urge someone to come with you, just saying *Viens!* – assuming you address them as *tu* – won't get them moving: you have to add a bit of emphasis by sticking an *Allez!* on the beginning – '*Allez! Viens!*' The resulting encouragement is thus a very firm way of saying, 'Come on! *Now!*' If you don't know the person very well, but still want them to come with you, you have to say, '*Allez! Venez!*' Either way, the resulting expression is self-contradicting: you are actually saying, 'Go! Come!' Nevertheless, it seems to work.

Tiens!

This is another term which is just that little bit deceptive because it can have two different meanings. *Tiens!* can be a simple, rather polite expression of surprise. When faced with something mildly unexpected – bumping into a friend in a shop or coming across something that you thought you had lost – you would just exclaim, '*Tiens!*' and raise your eyebrows a bit in the way that you might go, 'Oh!' in English. But *tiens* can also be the familiar, *tu* form of the imperative of the verb, *tenir*. In this context it means 'here!', or 'grab this', when passing something to someone. In the *vous* form, the imperative is *Tenez!* I used to get very confused when work colleagues, whom I generally called *vous*, suddenly said, '*Tiens!*', because I worried that they might be suddenly changing from *vouvoiement* to *tutoiement*. And I couldn't see what I was supposed to be grabbing hold of.

Chapeau!

When you want to congratulate someone on doing something well you can say *Bravo* as you would in English. You can also use the word *Bien!* to show your enthusiasm or approval for something. A third possibility is to congratulate someone using the word *Chapeau!* This, as you know, means 'hat' and the word is used as if to say, 'I take my hat off to you.' You can say *Chapeau!* to someone who has managed to do something you didn't think they could manage. Alternatively, you can use it to speculate on their chances of success, saying that, if they manage to do whatever it is, '*Moi, je lui dis "Chapeau!"*' – I'll say 'bravo!'.

C'est clair

A useful expression in that it doesn't really mean anything at all. In any conversation there comes a point where you have to reply to whatever the other person has just said in order to keep the conversation going. You might have no real idea what to say or any particular opinion to express, but want to show politely that you are still there, haven't died and are at least vaguely trying to follow what is being talked about. In English you would say something vague and meaningless like 'Absolutely', which doesn't advance the subject much but at least has the advantage of putting the burden back on the other person to keep things moving along. The equivalent French expression is *C'est clair*. This means, literally, 'that's clear', but in fact doesn't really mean much at all. It is best pronounced in as vacuous a tone as possible. As this is a fairly new expression, users tend to be quite young. They often leave their mouths open a bit afterwards to make it quite clear that no further opinion will be forthcoming.

Au secours!; À l'aide!

I thought it would be a good idea to include these two, mainly because, if they do ever come in useful, they will by their very nature come in very useful indeed. For they are the French way of calling 'Help!' They are used equally, although *Au secours!* seems to be used for situations that are a bit more dramatic than those where you cry, *À l'aide!* Both expressions have a useful common feature: that of a long vowel sound near the end. This is where you put the emphasis when the time comes to shout it out. Thus, you will cry, '*À l'aiiiiiide!*' or '*Au secouuuurs!*' with your mouth wide open. Failure to prolong the vowel sound will vastly reduce the chances of someone coming to your rescue. Another potentially useful term is *Au feu!* – 'fire!' All these expressions have a common feature: if you tried to create them simply by direct translation of the English equivalent, you would end up with *Aide!*, *Secours!* and *Feu!* which quite definitely wouldn't make anyone come to your assistance. You have to add the *Au . . .* or *À l' . . .* – to – at the beginning for it to work. It's a bit like the old English cry of 'to arms!'

Bof!

The theme of indifference seems to be a recurring one in French culture. We have had the shrug and now we are going to have the classic word to go with it. The word is *Bof!* For a simple, three-letter word, it can be imbued with a vast amount of feeling, depending on the circumstances in which it is used. A simple choice such as 'Do you want Cornflakes or Shreddies this morning?' would merit a short, relatively friendly '*Bof*', possibly followed by '*Ça m'est égal*' – I don't mind. But a tricky, potentially dangerous situation – 'How about going to see my parents again this weekend?' – can provoke a truly heartfelt, scathing *Bof!* which is more a dismissive expelling of breath than an actual word. When things get really tense, there can be a two-stage answer made up of a disabused exhalation of breath followed by the *Bof* itself. This sort of answer is definitely not a sign of enthusiasm. As with the 'tut tut' sound earlier on, it is important to keep your face immobile when you say *Bof!*

Sometimes, a simple *Bof* is not enough and you want to make clear exactly how indifferent you actually are. You could thus say,

'*Bof, je m'en fiche*' – I don't care – or, if you feel very strongly about your indifference, '*Bof, je m'en fous*' – I don't give a damn. Some people offer choices and suggest three possible replies: '*Et si on allait voir ma mère cet après-midi? Oui, non ou bof?*' – Shall we go and see my mother this afternoon? Yes, no or bof? In such cases, *bof* is often the safest answer.

Un ban!

I shall finish with a bit of clapping. At the end of a guided bus tour, when the guide was saying goodbye and trying to suggest that we give him a tip while doing his best not to actually use the word 'tip', one of the tour party suddenly called out, '*Allez: un ban pour le guide!*' At this, the whole bus – except me, for I had no idea what on earth was going on – launched into a burst of rhythmic clapping.

It went:

> Clap clap clap
> Clap clap clap
> Clap clap clap
> CLAP!

Everyone seemed to know the rhythm.

This sequence of rapid synchronized clapping is called *un ban* and is a common way of expressing gratitude or congratulations. The clapping sequence can, of course, vary from one region to another. In case you are at all interested, *un ban* was originally the term for the dramatic, rhythmic drum roll that used to come just before a royal proclamation was made.

6. L'année —
a French year

At the beginning of the book there was a brief overview of moments in a day that seem to be particularly French.

I am now going to repeat the process, writ large, and look at some key moments in a French year.

JOYEUX ANNIVERSAIRE

Even if you only come to France for a single day, you can be sure of being there on someone's birthday, though, of course, you will probably not know the someone in question.

Thus, it is quite probable that, however long or short a time you spend in France, you may spot some birthday greetings going on somewhere.

The French version of 'Happy birthday to you' is simply a direct French translation of the English song. The music and the repetitive structure are exactly the same as the English version, so, once you know that 'happy birthday' is *joyeux anniversaire*, you have the whole song at your fingertips.

It goes:

> *Joyeux anniversaire*
> *Joyeux anniversaire*
> *Joyeux anniversaire cher/chère [Insert name here]*
> *Joyeux anniversaire*

Keen observers will notice that there is no equivalent of the 'to you' part. The French view is that it isn't necessary as everyone knows who they are singing to. And anyway, it wouldn't scan properly if there were any more words added.

Unfortunately, you can get too enthusiastic when it comes to singing the song. In a restaurant not long ago, when most people were finishing their meals and had generally drunk enough to have reached the happy state known in French as *en pleine forme*, the lights suddenly went out. Bleary voices, including ours, were heard cheerfully speculating that it must be someone's birthday and that a cake would shortly make an appearance. With very little encouragement, the whole restaurant broke into a lusty rendering of '*Joyeux anniversaire*' in a pleasant, but somewhat incoherent blend of speeds and keys. But no cake appeared. After we had all sung the song through twice, increasingly raucously, the manager appeared holding a torch and explained that it wasn't anybody's birthday; there had just been a power cut.

LE RÉVEILLON

The word *réveillon* is disconcertingly ambiguous. As well as referring to the huge meal that is eaten on 24 December, it also applies to the huge meal that is eaten on New Year's Eve. Only the context will help you guess which one is being talked about.

Being quite logical at heart, I will start with Christmas.

If you want to get an idea of the differences between a traditional Christmas meal in France and one in Britain, the best place to start is at a French casualty department on Christmas Eve. For the first important difference concerns the dishes that are eaten.

A clue to the dish in question lies in the fact that one of the most common injuries to take people to casualty from about six in the evening of 24 December is a stab wound to the palm of the left hand. This is not the result of some close contact rioting in the Parisian suburbs but of an injury sustained while opening an oyster. For a key element of a French Christmas meal is a good lot of oysters. The only drawback with such things – apart from the fact that each time I have tried one, I have been violently ill – is that you have to open them. Thus, the run-up to Christmas in France is generally made more interesting by the arrival of the latest oyster-opening gadget. These are much in demand because the traditional knife with a short, pointed and very sharp blade ends up, as we have seen, stuck in the user's palm as often as in the interior of an oyster.

Palm-saving gadgets have included a vibrating electric knife that is supposed to force its way more easily through an oyster's defences, and a short bit of shiny wire that is intended to cut through the hinge bit that holds the oyster shut. Unfortunately, the disadvantage of the bit of wire is that you have to persuade the oyster to open up on an earlier occasion in order to insert the wire in advance. In my experience, oysters rarely cooperate in this activity.

Those who don't like oysters or, more probably, those who value the palm of their left hand, go for generous quantities of smoked salmon as a starter to their meal. An alternative, or often additional, starter is a good chunk of foie gras served with toast and a sweet white wine such as Sauternes. Unfortunately, foie gras generally turns out to be nearly as hard to open as an oyster in that it tends to come in a hermetically sealed glass jar. If you are ever faced with this sort of jar, you should organize a team of two to open it: one to grip the body of the jar as firmly as possible in both hands and the other to heave with all their strength on the tab of the orange rubber seal round the lid. If you can, try to be the one holding the jar because the tab has been known to tear off, flinging the puller backwards across the kitchen.

An important difference between the French and British Christmas meals lies in the dates on which they are consumed. A British Christmas meal is eaten, by definition, on Christmas Day, 25 December. Some people opt for having it at lunchtime; others prefer to eat in the evening. Whichever time is preferred, the date is always the same. In France, for reasons that have never been satisfactorily explained, many families have their meal on the evening of the 24th. Does this mean that they have another meal on Christmas Day? – I hear you ask. Well, no. Christmas Day in these French homes is a fairly cheerless affair which is spent recovering from the excesses of the night before. But what about the presents? As far as I know, many families exchange their presents just after the meal on Christmas Eve. However, as the meal is a very long and serious business, you are not going to open your first present much before midnight. In order to avoid impatience getting out of hand, some families allow one present to be opened by each family member at a point during the meal – for example, between the cheese and the pudding.

And a final word of advice: a taste for Christmas pudding is apparently not something that can be acquired by anyone who hasn't been born and raised in the UK, and is quite definitely not one that can be acquired if you are French. This is the case even if one of your parents is English.

LA SAINT SYLVESTRE

In the French calendar, every day of the year is associated with a respective saint. The feast day of Saint Sylvestre falls on 31 December and the last day of the year is referred to as *la Saint Sylvestre* rather than some equivalent of New Year's Eve.

On la Saint Sylvestre people have their second réveillon to usher in the New Year. This will be another huge meal including some or all of the following: oysters, foie gras, smoked salmon, a roast of some sort, a selection of cheese, a chocolatey dessert and lots of wine. Champagne, of course, is served at the stroke of midnight whereupon everybody launches into a veritable festival of shaking of hands, kissing of cheeks and wishing each other *Bonne année*.

The general rule of *réveillons* seems to be that you have Christmas with your family, or your family-in-law, and New Year with your friends.

'BONNE ANNÉE'

You might suppose that after all the celebratory shaking and kissing that goes on at *la Saint Sylvestre*, you could go back to work a couple of days later and everything would be normal. In fact no useful work gets done in France at all on the first morning of the year.

In my office, it usually starts with our receptionist. When I am barely over the office threshold, bleary and tired from the excesses of *le réveillon*, she will fling herself at me and launch into the New

Year four-bise routine. This starts with '*Bonne année, Charles*' and goes on, to the rhythm of the four kisses, '*Bonne année. Bonne santé. Plein de bonnes choses. Surtout, bonne santé*' – Happy New Year. Good health. Loads of good things. And especially good health. If you aren't familiar with the words you can generally get away with just mumbling, '*Oui! Bonne année*' a couple of times because whoever it is will be so engrossed in their routine that they won't realize that you aren't giving the standard response. I will then stagger away from the reception area and make my way round the rest of the office. All my women colleagues will go through exactly the same routine. They do this to all our colleagues, men or women, pretty much regardless of day-to-day office hierarchies. Even if you are usually a two-kiss person, you often become a four-kiss person for the duration of New Year.

Despite the fact that New Year is a very special occasion, my male colleagues thankfully won't try to do la bise to me. Instead they go through the New Year bloke's routine in which they each clasp my hand, grip my upper arm with their left hand and recite exactly the same greeting as the receptionist, pumping my hand to the rhythm of the routine. With experience you start to get the hang of it and manage to slip in a *Bonne santé* here or a *Plein de bonnes choses* there, all of which will make you feel quite authentic. Greeting each colleague is astonishingly time-consuming because, after the shaking and kissing, you have to tell each other, in great detail, what you ate and drank at *le réveillon*.

LA GALETTE DES ROIS

One could also be excused for assuming that returning to work after New Year would put an end to all the overeating and drinking for a while. Such an assumption would be understandable anywhere else but not in France.

It typically happens just after lunch on the Friday after going back to work. It certainly did the first year it happened to me. I found myself in the biggest of the offices, slightly bemused and standing with all my colleagues around a table laden with bottles of cider, glasses, plates and a huge *galette des Rois*. Two golden cardboard crowns were also laid out beside the galette. A galette des Rois is a round, tart-like cake made up of layers of pastry with a marzipan filling. It is best served warm. While someone cut up the galette, glasses of cider were poured for everyone. A pleasant feeling of anticipatory calm was shattered when someone asked, '*Qui veut aller sous la table?*' – who wants to go under the table? This was not an office euphemism for anything. It was a serious question. The galette contains a *fève*, which means bean. This is usually a small porcelain figure of the baby Jesus. Each galette has such a figure hidden in it somewhere, much like a coin in a Christmas pudding, and the lucky person who finds it is proclaimed king as a tribute to the visit of the Three Wise Men at Epiphany. Because you can often spot the fève lurking between two cut slices, the slices have to be allocated by someone who can't see them. Thus, one person puts each slice on a plate while another says who it is for. It is this other, impartial slice-attributing person who traditionally has to go under the table. If you are British, experiencing your first galette party, and have never imagined that anyone could possibly be asked to crawl under a table in an office environment, let alone in front of all your assembled colleagues, the shock and embarrassment of being nominated to do so are appalling. It takes long minutes to understand what is being asked, to be convinced that it really is up to you to do it because you are *le petit dernier* – the latest young person to join the company, and finally that the whole thing is not some elaborate joke. About the only thing that can be said for it is that you do get an unusual and close view of your colleagues' legs which is surprisingly agreeable. You are also treated to a warm round of applause when you finally come back out.

Whoever gets the fève will become king or queen, will have to wear the golden crown for the rest of the day, and will also have to choose a queen or king to join them. Being picked as king by a colleague who is queen is a useful measure of how you are viewed in the office. Unfortunately, there are some miserable spoilsports who can't face all this fuss and who, if they spot the fève in their slice, will try to hide it, or in some cases even swallow it, just to remain anonymous. Having done so, they shamelessly join in the collective grumbling about the useless *patissier* who seemingly forgot to put in the fève.

POISSON D'AVRIL

The notion of April Fool exists in France but there are two major differences. One of these definitely favours French people visiting the UK, rather than the reverse. In the UK you can only fool someone until midday: any attempt to fool someone after that time is deemed to make the fooler the fool (though I have never understood how that works in practice). In France you can fool anyone all day long. This came as a shock on my first experience of 1 April in France when, at around two in the afternoon, I had assumed that everything had finished and had dropped my guard completely, I was sneakily tricked by my brothers- and sisters-in-law. Crying, '*Mais, ce n'est pas juste – on ne peut pas faire ça en Angleterre*' – that's not fair: you can't do that in England – fell on cruelly deaf ears. Conversely, French visitors to the UK in early April will find themselves inexplicably free of attempts to fool them halfway through the day and will thus waste much nervous energy warding off threats that are in fact non-existent.

The second difference lies in the name – *poisson d'avril* – April fish. In France, rather than actually dupe someone, you can try to stick a small paper fish on their back to mark them as a fool. Children spend 31 March carefully cutting out paper fish shapes and, if they are artistic, decorating them with fins and gills. They then spend the whole of the next day trying to stick the fish on any innocent passer-by's back with a bit of sticky tape. Fish-sticking preliminaries are usually very easy to spot: a small child will suddenly urge you to look out of the window at some improbable thing, or will spend a lot of time casually sidling behind you, whistling innocently. That such children enjoy some degree of success is shown by the number of people, notably adults, whom you can see adorned with paper fishes on commuter trains and even in the office.

If you come to France on 1 April, it really is advisable to check your back regularly.

'JOYEUSES PÂQUES'

When I was a child, my Easter eggs used to be given by my parents. Other children's eggs were brought by the Easter Bunny or, in one case, by an entity called The Easter Man. French Easter eggs – *les œufs de Pâques* – are traditionally thought to be brought by *les cloches* – the bells. How bells can bring Easter eggs remains a mystery to me. What's more, to do the actual delivering, the bells are supposed to fly. I mean, really! Flying bells? But fly they do because everybody knows that, having delivered all the eggs, the bells (which are presumably church bells) then fly off to Rome. It is all very peculiar. What's more, no one ever says when the bells come back. However, it does lead to a seasonal French joke. If someone meets you shortly after Easter they may ask, '*Mais, vous n'êtes pas à Rome?*' – but aren't you in Rome? When you ask why they should think you are in Rome when you are clearly standing in front of them, they will reply, '*Parce que à Pâques, toutes les cloches vont à Rome.*' They think this is hilarious because *cloches* can mean either 'bells' or 'idiots'.

Once the bells have delivered the eggs to your house, you can't start eating them straight away. You first have to hide them around the house or garden and then get your children to look for them. Of course, you don't use big chocolate eggs full of chocolate buttons for this: it would be far too easy to find them. You use small foil-wrapped eggs which are the size of marbles. These can be really tricky to find. When we moved out of our flat some time ago we found three ageing chocolate eggs that had been too well hidden at some previous Easter.

Finally, a distinct disadvantage of Easter celebrations in France is that Good Friday is not a public holiday.

LA FÊTE DE LA MUSIQUE

We met some British people recently who exclaimed at length about the wonderful weekend they had just spent in France. 'It was fabulous!' they enthused. 'There was music in the streets everywhere we went. We can't wait to go back.' At this, we stunned them by correctly guessing that they had been there on 21 June. It was an easy deduction because 21 June is the day of the annual *fête de la musique* – the national music festival. This first took place on 21 June 1982 thanks to the efforts of the culture minister of the day, Jack Lang. The date was chosen as it is the summer solstice – the longest day. The original slogan was *faites de la musique* – go out and make music – which sounds just like *fête de la musique*. The festival is extremely popular and has spread rapidly throughout France. Now, wherever you go on the evening of 21 June, you are sure to come across a formal concert or a group of amateurs playing in the street for fun. In the bigger cities every district has its own concert.

LES SOLDES

Imagine for a moment that you have a shop – it can sell whatever you like – somewhere in France. Business hasn't been too brisk lately so you decide to have a sale to boost your profits a bit. What can be wrong with that? Everything. Like a wide variety of things in France, sales in shops are strictly regulated. Article L-310-3 of the French commercial code clearly defines when *les soldes* – sales – can take place. Only two periods are allowed: one at the beginning of January, the other in late June. Les soldes can last a maximum of six weeks and the dates are fixed by local government decree. After a couple of weeks, some sale prices are cut for a second time. This is known as *deuxième démarque*. Some people put off buying things in the first week or so, saying, '*J'attends la deuxième démarque.*' Of course, shops are allowed to have special offers, or have sales campaigns, outside the prescribed periods. But these can't be called *soldes*. These sales campaigns often seem to have completely misleading names. The BHV department store chain likes having a special promotion called *les 6 jours du BHV*. This apparent six-day special actually lasts a couple of weeks.

Once the summer sales are over, it's time to go away on holiday.

LES GRANDES VACANCES

All French employees enjoy five weeks' holiday a year, at least three of which will be taken in July or August. You might well imagine that the only vocabulary you will need to talk about holidays will be simple phrases such as *aller à la plage*.

For a start, the French don't go away to the beach; they go away to the seaside – '*aller à la mer*'. But much more interesting is the vocabulary you will need to talk about what they do when they get there.

Décompresser

French people, and here perhaps I mostly mean Parisians, believe themselves to be stressed due to overwork. Some of them undoubtedly are. All the others probably aren't: their irascible behaviour comes not from stress but simply from the fact that they are Parisian, in other words, naturally irritable. Nevertheless, the fact that everyone believes that they are stressed lies behind the principal French objective when they go away on holiday. People go away to *décompresser* – de-stress or unwind. It is a good word because, when you use it, you make clear how overworked you would like people to believe you have been recently, thus, with any luck, getting a bit of respect and admiration from your peers.

Farniente

But how exactly does one *décompresser*? That's easy: by doing something called *farniente*. This handy Italian term has been adopted with great enthusiasm by the French because they previously lacked a word for just doing nothing at all, preferably while covered in suntan oil. *Faire du farniente sur la plage* refers to the blissful, but possibly not very stimulating pastime of lounging around doing nothing at all on a beach, generally in close proximity to a large number of other people who are similarly employed and are listening to ghetto blasters. French travel guides often recommend certain beaches as being particularly suited to *amateurs de farniente*, a term that can cause confusion: *amateurs* in this context refers to those who like something rather than those who do things rather less well than professionals.

Lézarder

If this *farniente* business sounds a bit too strenuous, there is another handy word for lounging on a sun-soaked beach – *lézarder*. This literally means to bask in the sun like a lizard and perfectly describes the way people on beach holidays lie quite still while soaking up dangerous quantities of rays. The term is particularly appropriate given the slightly reptilian, scaly look of such people's skin when they get older.

Flâner

If you don't like beaches but still want to *décompresser*, you can devote part or all of your holiday to an activity known as *flâner*. This describes the pleasant holiday activity of just wandering along streets, looking at whatever it is you are passing – shops, market stalls or nice buildings – but not really doing much about it. If you get the pace right, *flâner* will let you *décompresser* just as well as a bit of *farniente* while having the advantage of keeping you away from all those ghetto blasters. It is also better for your skin.

Chassé-croisé

One of the disadvantages to summer holidays in France is that everyone seems to go away at precisely the same time, notably because the holiday home rentals always go from Saturday to Saturday. This leads to the infamous *journées rouges* when the roads from Paris to the south are jammed with cars. However, there are one or two weekends in late July or mid-August where the roads are especially busy in both directions, to and from Paris.

This is because one lot of people are setting off for the south while those who were blocking the roads two or three weeks earlier are now returning, bronzed, poorer and irritable, to the Paris area. This produces *un chassé-croisé* or mass to-ing and fro-ing of cars. If you are in France on such a weekend, it is probably a good idea to stay on the beach or in bed. The one place you really don't want to be is the Vallée du Rhône – the area around Lyons – which is the ultimate bottleneck on French roads. Traffic jams there are so notorious that they only get a mention on the news if they are more than 60 kilometres long and last at least five hours. The only good thing about *chassé-croisé* weekends is that, as everyone is stuck in a jam somewhere, it is a great time to visit Paris, which is really quiet.

'LA BOULANGERIE EST FERMÉE'

As all of France seems to go on holiday at the same time it is common to find yourself faced with a shop which is closed for the holiday period. In most shops, all you will see is a little card in the window informing you that the shop is shut and that it will reopen on a certain date around the end of August.

Such casual information would not be at all acceptable for bakers. *Une boulangerie* is such a key part of French life that many aspects of its operation are subject to strict regulations.

For a start, the term used to define what sort of baker's shop you are standing outside is clearly regulated and there seems to be a definite hierarchy in the names used.

The best sort of baker is a *boulangerie artisanale* or crafts-man baker. If you have one of these nearby, you will have to be prepared to queue on busy days. Indeed, there are some boulangeries artisanales that are considered to be so special that at weekends you will often see a queue that extends along the pavement. The fact that the people queuing came to the shop prepared for a long wait is shown by the number who pass the time reading books or magazines.

Next comes the conventional boulangerie whose bread will still be very good. All things not being equal, there will be little things that will make customers believe that a given baker is a little bit better or fractionally worse than a neighbouring one. This is just enough to make or break its reputation in the eyes of the locals. Once a baker has a good reputation, people will generally make that little extra effort to buy their bread there rather than using a nearer one.

The lowest in the hierarchy is quite definitely a *dépôt de pain*. This is a shop selling bread which is not made on the premises by the proprietor but brought in from a central supplier. Such shops are acceptable if you desperately need some bread, but are generally viewed with deep suspicion by bread aficionados. Such people consider the sign *dépôt de pain* as a sort of apology.

As bakers are considered to form so vital a part of French life, they can only close on approved dates that are coordinated with other nearby bakers. This means that in the window of a baker's shop that is closed for the holiday you will find a card giving the names and addresses of nearby bakers that are open. Some shops even have a helpful little map.

While the notice is fairly formal there is occasionally a handwritten note at the bottom that adds a personal touch, saying something like, *Toute l'équipe est partie à la mer pour se dorer au soleil* – all the team has gone to the seaside together to get brown.

LES OBJETS ENCOMBRANTS

This isn't really an annual event at all but deserves a mention nonetheless. Once a month the local council organizes the collection of *les objets encombrants* – things that you want to throw away but which are too big to be taken by the *éboueurs* – the ordinary refuse collection. This event is known in our household as 'big rubbish night'. You know it is big rubbish night because, from about six on a Sunday evening, little white vans driven by tough, shifty looking people, often accompanied by their husbands, start driving round the local streets. They are looking for treasures that have been thrown out. As we live in a nice suburb to the west of Paris, people don't just chuck away broken beds, watering cans with holes in them or empty tins of paint. They get rid of some surprising and often expensive stuff. Walking round the village, nosing in the piles outside other people's houses is thus a popular and often productive pastime. Past successes for us include: the gas cooker we used for two years; a video camera (complete with a nice film of the previous owner's daughter coming second in a ballet competition); and a splendid racing bike just like my old one that was stolen when I was sixteen. Because there are such treasures to be found, you have to watch out for the white van people, who have been known to come to blows over finds.

7. Les formalités – the formal side of things

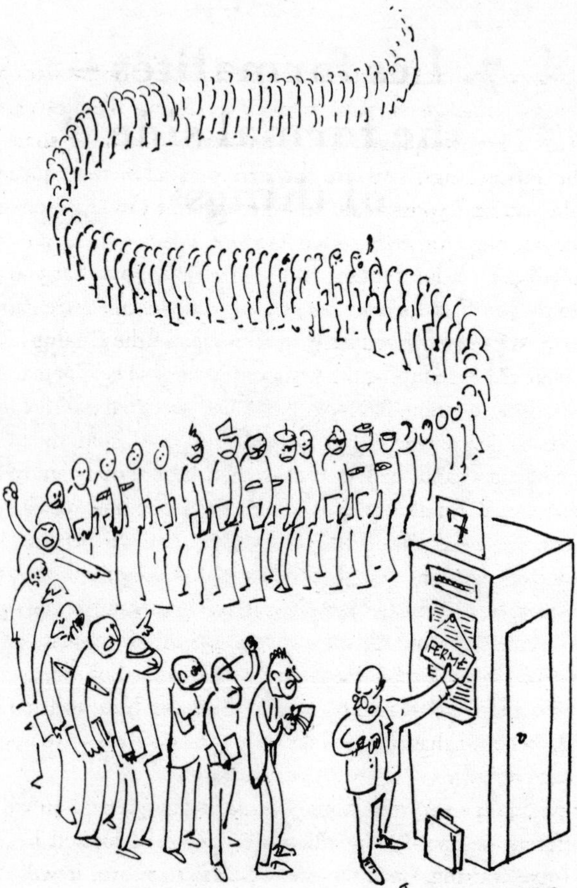
7
FERMÉ

The discovery that the French are an intensely formal nation may come as a shock to anyone who's ever found themselves in the thick of a French queue. This is especially true if, at some point in the proceedings, you are the first person in that queue. For should you find yourself the first person at a bus stop, or outside a cinema, and you form what George Mikes called 'an orderly queue of one', it is vital that you realize right now that you aren't going to stay first for very long. Nor will the queue remain very orderly. We once arrived early at a cinema in the Champs Elysées and were delighted to be the first people there. The cinema, knowing all about queuing habits in Paris, had installed parallel lines of barriers to define where the queue should be. Despite the presence of the barriers, and the fact that we had been closely studying the posters stuck on the cinema doors at the moment when they opened, we were astonished to discover that we were no longer first and second when we reached the ticket counter, but sixteenth and nineteenth. What's more, it was obvious that the only people who seemed to find this in any way odd or unjust were us. Everybody else, notably the fifteen people ahead of me, as well as the two that had managed to slip between Inès and me, quite clearly believed that this was the only reasonable way to approach a ticket counter.

If you happen to start further back in the queue, you will have a different perspective on things. Whatever it looked like while you were waiting, once the queue starts to move, it will rapidly transform itself into a cross between a rugby scrum and a street fight. As in the previous example, as soon as the queue moves forward, *you* will instantly find yourself a whole lot further back than you had been.

Of course, long before the queue starts to advance, you will be constantly losing ground to all those people who are convinced that their place is much nearer the front of the queue than yours. Pushing in is widely viewed simply as an expression of the true essence of queuing.

So what should you do about it? Remonstrate? Threaten violence? Of course not: you aren't French. You are free to try, but no good will come of it. The only thing to do is to try to view the whole thing as though you were David Attenborough making a documentary about the social habits of a strange, recently dis-covered tribe. I find this strategy very calming and occasionally I even find myself providing a suitable commentary out loud when faced with extreme examples of queue-jumping.

Sadly, this technique doesn't work particularly well when you are faced with the rules and regulations that underlie most aspects of French life. These prove every bit as hard for a foreigner to get their head around as French queue-forming habits. For instance, you can't just sign your name to a formal document in France.

Filling in papers is so easy in the UK: you can complete any form, whether to take out an insurance policy, open a savings account or apply for a mortgage, and just sign your name at the bottom. Completing any such document in France requires more from the signatory than a simple signature. Any formal signature has to be prefixed with the handwritten words, *Lu et approuvé* – read and approved. This is peculiar because reading and approv-ing is exactly what you won't do. When the bank clerk or the *notaire* – solicitor – pushes a multi-page document towards you and asks you to sign, the last thing you are going to do is wade through all the impenetrable legal French to see whether you accept all the terms and conditions. What you are in fact going to do is hold the pen a few centimetres above the paper, stick your bottom lip out a bit in a reflective sort of way, nod your head knowledgeably while frowning just a little, hope for the best and then sign the thing.

At all levels things formal in France are quite different from those in the UK.

PRÉSIDENT DE LA RÉPUBLIQUE

It would be wrong to assume that the president of France is just known as *le président*. To call him this would be a slight not only on him but also on the whole of France. He should be addressed as *Monsieur le Président de la République*, or, at the very least, *Monsieur le Président*, and is announced or introduced as such each time he makes a speech to the nation on the TV. Any presidential speech to the nation is notable for the number of times that *La France* is mentioned, generally in an emotional or reverential tone of voice. If you think back to any speech to the British nation, the name of the country very rarely gets a mention. On the other side of the Channel, not only is France mentioned, but speeches are specifically directed to French men and French women and may thus begin with the words '*Françaises, français . . .*' or, at the very least, will include the words at some later point. Again, the name of the people will be pronounced in a particularly emotive way. This is something that you couldn't do in English even if you wanted to. A speaker is limited to saying something like 'People of Britain' which doesn't have anything like the emotional content of

'Françaises, français'. If he has used the words '*Françaises, français* ...' too often in a speech, the president may change and refer to '*Mes chers compatriotes* ...' – my dear compatriots – instead.

LE PREMIER MINISTRE

The president is the head of state and he is supported by the prime minister, who is usually expected to get on with the actual day-to-day running of the government. Interestingly, the role of the prime minister, and notably his public image, is a function of the character of the president. Jacques Chirac, who sometimes gave the impression that he would rather have been king than president, was happy to leave the work, and especially all the can-carrying, to a series of prime ministers, all of whom were constantly in the public eye. Nicolas Sarkozy, on the other hand, has a particularly hands-on approach and likes to do as much as possible himself. The prime minister is so upstaged by this that he is hardly ever seen on TV; indeed not everyone is really sure what he looks like.

LE PARLEMENT FRANÇAIS

In accordance with the Constitution of the Fifth Republic, the French parliament is made up of two houses: L'Assemblée Nationale – the lower house of parliament – comprises 577 members, known as *députés*, who are elected by national ballot every five years. This lower house meets in a building opposite the

Place de la Concorde known as Le Palais Bourbon. The upper house is Le Sénat and comprises 331 elected *sénateurs* who meet in the Palais du Luxembourg.

LIBERTÉ, ÉGALITÉ, FRATERNITÉ

The famous French motto dates back to the declaration of the Republic in 1790 after the French Revolution. It means, of course, Liberty, Equality, Brotherhood. France being France, all of the words making up the motto are clearly defined in legal texts. Apparently, nothing can be left to chance: everything has to be carefully and clearly codified. *Liberté* and *Égalité* are both defined in the *Déclaration des droits de l'homme et du citoyen* of 1793 – the Declaration of the rights of man and of citizens.

For example:

L'égalité consiste en ce que la loi est la même pour tous, soit qu'elle protège, soit qu'elle punisse. L'égalité n'admet aucune distinction de naissance, aucune hérédité de pouvoirs ...

As for Fraternité:

Ne faites pas à autrui ce que vous ne voudriez pas qu'on vous fît; faites constamment aux autres le bien que vous voudriez en recevoir ...

Despite all the long and formal definitions, most of this basically means, 'Do as you would be done by.'

LA CINQUIÈME RÉPUBLIQUE

France's current constitutional state is known as *La Cinquième République* – the fifth republic. This was brought into force by a new version of the constitution prepared by de Gaulle in September 1958. The main features of this republic, when compared to any of the earlier ones, lie in the amount of power that resides in the president and the way the president is elected by ballot.

But if this is the fifth republic, what happened to the previous four? The problem is that the four earlier republics didn't just follow one after the other. Indeed, rather than a simple series of republics, the period from the end of the absolute monarchy back in 1791 to the present fifth republic was filled with an ever-changing series made up of: the four republics; the first and second empires; a couple of periods of constitutional monarchy; the first and second restorations; and something called *les Cent Jours*. Of course, they weren't all in that order.

I would like to explain it more clearly, but I can't make much sense of it.

LE DRAPEAU TRICOLORE

The French national flag, with its three vertical bands of blue, white and red, dates back to Louis XVI when the traditional red and blue flag of Paris was combined with the white of the flag of the Bourbons. It was formally adopted as the national flag in 1794 and has been the symbol of France ever since, apart from during *les Cent Jours* and the second restoration of the monarchy. Of the colours, red was a traditional colour of standards and banners, while blue regularly featured in French royal standards and coats of arms. The colour white has religious roots and is seen as being the colour of divinity. The tones and intensities of the colours have varied over the years or with the circumstances in which the flag is used. The colours are now standardized, the blue being called Reflex Blue, which has a CMYK (don't ask) number of 100.70.0.5.

LES FLICS

The French apparent disregard for law and order is all the more surprising when you realize that there is not one national police force, but two. In the course of your travels you may thus encounter either an *agent de police* also known as a *policier*, or a *gendarme*.

A gendarme is employed by the Gendarmerie Nationale, which is a military organization run by the defence ministry. They are thus not civil employees but essentially soldiers. Their main role is to provide help and assistance, maintain order and deal with traffic control principally in rural and suburban areas.

Un agent de police is a member of the Police Nationale, which is a civil service organization run by the ministry of the interior. They have essentially the same duties as gendarmes but only ever deal with urban areas. Urban areas are considered to be cities having a population of over twenty thousand. In Paris, the policiers are helped out by the gendarmes.

Police cars are typically white while gendarmes travel in blue cars. Gendarmes also ride blue motorbikes or fly in blue heli-copters. They can even be seen on horseback, though the horses are rarely blue. Gendarmes used to be recognized by their *képi* but since 2004 they have changed to wearing more practical caps. Of course, whichever sort of police officer you are faced with, they will definitely be armed. The current pistol of choice is a Sig Sauer.

The Gendarmerie Nationale includes two well-known sub-divisions: la Garde Républicaine, who are charged with ensuring the president's safety, notably on ceremonial occasions, and the GIGN. This is the Groupe d'Intervention de la Gendarmerie Nationale, an elite force comprising 320 extremely fit and well-trained officers who are there to deal with any extreme situation. They are based in Versailles, which is reassuringly close to where we live.

In day-to-day life, it doesn't really matter which sort of police officer you deal with: if you are looking for their help, either one will be equally cooperative. Similarly, if they are looking for you, the result will be the same whoever stops you. Incidentally, if you are arrested by the police and held at the police station pending enquiries, you will be said to be held *en garde à vue*. Who knows when this expression may come in useful?

ARTICLE 1382

The rise of Napoleon Bonaparte led to many changes being made in France. One of the least visible, but possibly the most useful, was a formal codification of civil and criminal law. All the articles that make up, for example, 'Le Code Civil' – the French civil code

– date from the time of Napoleon. They are most often to be found in a series of bright red legal textbooks published by Dalloz which brighten the shelves of every lawyer's office.

It is said that Napoleon himself drafted many of the articles, several of which are splendid examples of succinct and lucid thinking. The best-known article of the civil code is Article 1382. This states: '*Tout fait quelconque de l'homme, qui cause à autrui un dommage, oblige celui par la faute duquel il est arrivé à le réparer*', which roughly translates as, 'Any act by man, which causes harm to another, obliges he whose fault it is to repair that harm.'

This article can be invoked in a whole range of day-to-day situations, from being knocked over by a bus to complaining about being kept awake by your neighbour's cockerel.

X – L'INCONNU

The letter X can be used in French not only to represent an unknown quantity as it is in English algebra but also to refer to *l'inconnu* – an unknown person or entity. This is shown by two common examples that appear frequently in the news.

Né sous X

French birth certificates include the names of both the child's parents. If a child is abandoned and the names of the parents are unknown, a capital letter X will be used in place of the parents' names. The child will have a name given by his or her adoptive parents but will be forever referred to in subsequent official documents as *Né sous X* – born to unnamed parents. It is estimated that currently some 400,000 such people are trying to find out the identity of at least one of their parents. Various associations and websites exist to help them in their search.

Plainte contre X

If you have in some way suffered at the hands of a third party and you want to take legal action in the hope of stopping whatever it is, getting the perpetrator punished or receiving some form of compensation, you have to file a complaint. This is known as 'porter plainte'. It is common on the news, or in day-to-day life, to hear about someone who has had an accident or who has been attacked or robbed and who announces formally whether or not they wish to 'porter plainte'. Having decided to go ahead and file a complaint – possibly invoking Article 1382 – you have to put it into action. This is called *déposer une plainte contre quelqu'un* – filing a formal complaint against someone. For minor problems you file your complaint at the police station; for major ones you file it before a court. But what happens if you have been wronged in some way by a party or parties unknown? If you don't know whom to file your complaint against, you have to file it as *une plainte contre X* – a complaint against an unknown party. This works both for unknown individuals and for unknown legal entities such as companies. You may think that there is no point in filing a complaint against someone unknown. However, filing such a complaint is necessary in many cases to get the legal ball rolling. If you haven't filed *une plainte* of any sort, you generally have no chance of getting any money from insurance companies or receiving any compensation.

SANS PAPIERS

Everyone in France has to have, and carry with them, *une pièce d'identité* – some sort of formal identity document such as an identity card – or a passport. Foreign nationals who take up residence in France have also to have a resident's permit. However, not all foreign visitors are able, or in some cases, willing, to obtain the necessary paperwork or to go through the long and complex procedures required to obtain their resident's permit. In some cases, such people don't even have a passport. People who continue to stay in France without the required ID or permit are said to be *en situation irrégulière* – in an illegal situation – and are known in the media reports as *sans papiers* – without the necessary papers. This may well sound surprisingly dramatic and even reminiscent of wartime situations but it is all too common to see reports on the news of buildings inhabited by groups of foreign residents who have absolutely no formal documents and who run the risk of being arrested and deported. In recent years such deportations have become increasingly common. People who are *sans papiers* nevertheless manage to hold down unofficial jobs, typically in the restaurant or the construction industries. This is because, while they don't have the necessary papers to stay in the country, they can still sign on to the social security and even pay their income tax. On one occasion, these unofficial workers went on strike to draw attention to their plight and to try to speed up the issue of their long-awaited papers.

CHEZ LE MÉDECIN

Going to the doctor in France seems quite civilized compared to
the descriptions I hear of visits to surgeries in the UK. Having
made an appointment with your *médecin traitant* – GP – you turn
up and spend a brief time waiting in a room that is generally
pleasant, well furnished and often has music playing softly in
the background. As many GPs seem to work on their own, there
is rarely a receptionist so the doctor will come and fetch you in
person. Handshakes will of course be exchanged, the doctor being
greeted with, '*Bonjour, docteur.*' What visitors to France find the
most surprising is that at the end of the consultation, which will
have been pleasant and unrushed, you will be expected to pay.
Any visit to a medical practitioner or a dentist requires payment
to be made by the patient. This is why it is now common to see
credit-card readers on a doctor's desk. In the old days, paying was
a slow and complex process: you had to fill in forms that you
would later send off to the social security so as to be reimbursed
for all or part of the cost of the consultation. Nowadays, almost
everyone has a *carte vitale*. This is a bright green credit card bearing the words *carte d'assurance maladie* (I've got mine here in
front of me) – medical insurance card – together with your name
and social security number. The doctor puts the card in the reader
at the time of payment and this sends all the details of the consultation directly to the social security. The form filling is no longer
necessary and the reimbursement appears in your bank a week or
so later. It is all remarkably efficient and pain-free.

NON-ASSISTANCE ...

Most laws punish someone for *doing* something. There is a provision in French penal law that punishes people for *not* doing something. Article 223-6 of the French Penal Code relates to an act referred to as *Non-assistance à personne en danger*. In order for the article to apply, you have to be aware that there is a danger to someone, be in a position to do something about it, and not be put into danger yourself by doing whatever is necessary. The article applies not only to doctors or nurses but to anyone who witnesses a situation requiring some form of action. This action can be limited to calling the police or the fire brigade but it can be expected to go further than that if there is no other help to be had. Stopping to take photos of Princess Diana's car crash but not giving any first aid was considered to be *non-assistance à personne en danger*. This is also expressed by the notion of *l'obligation de porter secours* where a witness to any form of accident is required to provide assistance or first aid to the best of their ability.

LA LOI DE ...

Not all laws are defined by the French penal or civil codes. One that isn't, but which is extremely well known, is the so-called *loi de l'emmerdement maximal*. The key word, *emmerdement*, which is clearly a derivative of the word *merde*, roughly means 'a bloody mess'. Thus, the law states that of all possible situations or outcomes, the one that happens will be the one that causes the biggest mess or the worst problems. This is even more pessimistic than the British 'sod's law', which merely states that if anything can go wrong, it will.

8. Le sport – the French and sport

So, which country invented football? Why, England of course, in 1863.

And who came up with the idea of picking up the ball and running with it? The English (whether or not you believe the story of William Webb Ellis at Rugby).

What about cricket?

And golf? Or curling?

Even the idea of skiing downhill fast for fun, rather than just using skis to get about the place in wintertime?

The majority of modern sports are generally believed to have been invented or popularized by the British.

What is more interesting is that two things generally happen after the British have invented a new game and have taught people throughout the world how to play it. The first thing is all too obvious: practically everyone learns to play whatever game it is better than the British and promptly thrashes them in any competitive event.

The second thing is less well known.

To see what it is, let's go back to football. Once the British had codified the rules of association football and taught everyone else how to play it, there was a need for a competition if only to prove that everyone else could play it better. With this in mind, a Frenchman called Jules Rimet came up with a splendid idea in 1930 to hold something called a Football World Cup. The gold cup that the Brazilians, Germans, Italians and French like to hold aloft at four-year intervals was called the Jules Rimet Cup in his honour.

Then there is the Euro football competition which was also

devised by the French. Indeed, football's governing body FIFA was a French idea. It was founded in Paris in 1904, the letters standing for Fédération Internationale de Football Association.

Then we come to Baron de Coubertin, a Frenchman. In 1894 he founded the International Olympic Committee with a view to holding the first Olympic Games of the modern era in Athens in 1896.

The British were active in developing high-speed motor cars that were raced from the beginning of the last century. But who came up with the idea of an international governing body to manage motor sport? The FIA – the Fédération Internationale d'Automobile – was founded in Paris in 1904, the same year as the French founded FIFA. The Automobile Club de l'Ouest also envisaged the first major endurance motor race in 1923. The idea seems to have been popular because the Le Mans twenty-four-hour race is still going strong.

What about sailing? The great transatlantic races such as the America's Cup clearly weren't a French idea. The ultimate yacht race that involves one person on one boat going all the way round the world in one go clearly was. It is called Le Vendée Globe and was the brainchild of Philippe Jeantot in 1989.

The French didn't just spend the twentieth century coming up with international competitions or founding governing bodies: they also developed some impressive national sporting events. A year before FIA and FIFA were conceived the French had the idea of a huge national cycle race. The Tour de France has fascinated the nation, and much of the world, ever since. Sadly, while the French devised the Tour de France they haven't won it very often. Like anyone else, however, they do like to have national heroes for any given sport. These two facts explain the fame of Raymond

Poulidor. Poulidor is astonishingly well known in the world of cycling despite the fact that he never won a great cycle race, though he did come second rather a lot. Indeed he is famous mainly for the fact that he very often nearly won, but didn't quite. He came second in the Tour de France in 1964, 1965 and 1974. He also came second in the world cycling championships in 1974, second in the Trophée Baracchi in 1966 and second in the Tours–Versailles race of 1976. His name has come to be used for anyone who comes second in something, whatever the field of activity.

And one last one before we move on – the Dakar rally, which was originally called the Paris–Dakar when it was founded by a Frenchman in 1979.

Thus, while the British are proud because they invent games, the French also have reasons to be proud because they can be relied upon either to form a useful governing body or to come up with a really good competition to see who is best at whatever game the British have just invented.

INDIVIDUALISTE?

There are those who believe that if you were asked to list the less flattering components of the French character you would have to include the fact that it is often perceived to be selfish or, perhaps more generously, individualistic. This view doesn't stand up so well when you consider French successes at certain team-based sporting events. For the French are generally pretty good at team sports. Indeed, they regularly reach the final rounds of competitions involving football, rugby, basketball, handball, volleyball and more.

More interestingly, the French are also good at team events that are founded on individual performances. Take tennis for example. The French regularly have several players in the list of the top-twenty best players in the world. However, these players tend to do even better in team events like the Davis Cup. France has won this nine times, fewer than the USA or Australia of course, but as often as Great Britain.

Finally, the individualistic side of the supposed French character also tends to disappear when it comes to team events in athletics. While French individual athletes don't always win medals, their relay teams, which include the same individual athletes, do better than might be expected in races such as the 4×100-metre or 4×400-metre relays.

And on this paradox, that I am not yet able to satisfactorily explain, I shall move on to the French reluctance to swim the Channel.

LA MANCHE

The first thing to note about the body of water between Dover and Calais is that it is perceived differently from opposite sides. The English lay claim to it by referring to it as the English Channel whereas the French show their indifference by just calling it 'La Manche' – the sleeve. Indeed I have just checked the handy little map in my French diary and it seems to care so little about the water in question that it doesn't even bother to give it a definite article; it is shown simply as Manche.

The importance of the Channel for the English perhaps lies in the fact that if you want to visit the nearest foreign country you have no choice but to cross it. It is a lot easier in France: there are a good half-dozen countries that you can reach without having to risk getting your feet wet.

This fascination with 'abroad' starting on the other side of the Channel may well explain the English passion for crossing it in various ways. As soon as anyone comes up with a new way of moving around, and looks for a way to see how far they can do it, they tend to think of the English Channel. Not only will crossing it provide a good test of whatever it is, it will also take you all the way to a foreign country.

Thus, the first person to swim the Channel was Matthew Webb on 25 August 1875. He swam from England to France and took 21 hours and 45 minutes.

An extremely long time then went by before anyone on the other side felt the need to swim back in the opposite direction. The first person to do so – in 1923 – was Enrico Tiraboschi, who, as his name suggests, was not French. The first French person to swim across was apparently Georges Michels in September 1926, fifty-one years after Webb's first swim.

One French person who showed great enthusiasm for getting across the Channel was Louis Blériot. He flew across in his Blériot XI aeroplane on 25 July 1909, taking a mere 37 minutes. He was inspired to do this, not because 'it was there', or because he particularly wanted to visit England, but because Britain's *Daily Mail* had offered a prize of 25,000 francs to the first person to do so.

PÉTANQUE

The game of *pétanque* deserves a mention notably because, if you list French sports by the number of members of a recognized club who play them, *pétanque* is up in seventh place. It comes just behind football, tennis, judo, horse riding, basketball and golf – the principal sports at which the French do well on the world stage. France has won the *pétanque* world championship (in which several other countries are also allowed to take part) twenty-three times. While nearly 400,000 club members play *pétanque* regularly, millions more play casually, often during their summer holidays.

A brief reminder of the rules may be useful. You can play in teams of one or two players with three *boules* each, or three players with two *boules* each. Each player stands inside a circle some 50 cm in diameter and throws his boules towards *le cochonnet* – the jack, a small ball that has been thrown 6 to 10 metres from the circle. Players in turn throw their boules, trying to get as close as possible to the jack. At the end of the round, the team with the boule closest to the jack wins and scores a number of points equal to the number of boules nearer to the jack than the opponent's nearest ball.

If you watch a *pétanque* game you will hear two frequently used terms: *tirer* and *pointer*. These are often used in a question from one player to another: '*Tu tires, ou tu pointes?*' *Pointer* is the act of making a precision throw, aiming to get as close to the jack as possible. *Tirer* is an aggressive act, trying to bomb an opponent's boule and knock it as far away as possible. *Tirer* is thus a whole lot more fun than *pointer*. The only disadvantage of opting to *tirer* is that if you miss the opponent's ball, your boule will fly off into the distance and has no chance of scoring a point. It is remarkably easy to tell the difference between a success at *pointer* and someone who has just succeeded in *tirer*. In one, a ball rolls silently up to the jack; in the other there is a loud clang and boules fly off at speed in all directions. Typically, a *pointeur* will choose a ball which is a little heavier than one used by a seasoned *tireur*. One thing that pleases me greatly when watching a *pétanque* game is seeing how many of the players are too lazy, or too stiff, to bend down and pick up their boules. Such people have a strong magnet on the end of a piece of string that they use to fish them up with.

ON A GAGNÉ!

French supporters don't seem to stick little plastic flags on their car roof before an important match involving the national team. Indeed, nothing much happens at all beforehand. However, they make up for this afterwards. An important sporting victory is usually followed by intense scenes of national rejoicing. Scant minutes from the final whistle, flag-bedecked cars will appear from nowhere filled with fans with tricolore-painted faces. But the best bit of such celebrations is the hooting. For you can't celebrate anything properly in France without a good bit of hooting of horns. And there is a special technique to it that has to be learnt. Of course, you can just lean out of your car window and shout to express your joy, but it is so much better if you tap out the French victory rhythm on your horn. This consists of two short hoots followed by two longer hoots. This represents the syllables of the victory chant: *On a gagné* – we won.

For example, during the recent Rugby World Cup which was held in France, the French team met the redoubtable All Blacks in the quarter-finals. To everyone's astonishment and delight – well, everyone who supported the French, that is – and against all expectations, France actually beat the New Zealanders. Beating New Zealand at rugby is up there with beating Brazil at football. Barely minutes after the final whistle, huge numbers of fans took to the streets to celebrate the win in the time-honoured way, even though it was only the quarter-final.

As well as the traditional hooting and chanting of *On a gagné* there were chants to mock the losers such as:

> *Et, ils sont où?*
> *Et, ils sont où?*
> *Et, ils sont où les néo-zélandais?*
> [Where are the New Zealanders now?]

This is a revised version of *Et ils sont où les brésiliens?* which gets chanted after every football victory over the team from Brazil. It is a good chant but the original scans considerably better than *les néo-zélandais*.

LA LIESSE

We had watched the France–All Blacks match with some young friends, Laura and Chris, who were over from England. As they had never witnessed *la liesse*, as French collective sporting rejoicing is known, we piled them into the car and set off to the local town, hooting the two shorts and two long hoots all the while. After abandoning the car, we continued on foot through streets full of hooting cars and their flag-waving passengers, some of whom were even sitting on the roof. Each time a hooting car passed us, the passengers gave a victory yell, then looked at us expectantly, waiting for us to cry something in return. Not having had time to master all the appropriate chants, Laura and Chris worried about what they should yell in order to appear as French as possible. We told them to limit themselves to a simple, all-purpose *Ouaaiiis!* – a long, drawn-out form of *oui* that is a bit like an American 'Yaaayy!'

It worked a treat. Their every '*Ouaaiiis!*' to passing cars was masterful and they used it to great effect when coming face to face with fans who were on foot. Not one fan spotted that they weren't French.

An ability to yell *Ouaaiiis!* convincingly is the sort of thing that is bound to come in useful one day, so I urge you to practise shouting it out right now, wherever you happen to be.

9. L'histoire française – important historical events

A question to start the chapter:

What do the following battles have in common? Furnes, Crécy, Comines, Agincourt (or Azincourt), Castillon, Waterloo.

Apart from the fact that they are all places in or near France, their common feature is that for one country they are sites of military prowess, while for another they are relatively unknown or even forgotten entirely, notably because that country fared considerably less well in the battles.

Any country's view of historical events is particularly subjective: they remember the bits that are important to them. That is why I thought it would be useful to look at a few typically French events in history, the sort of thing that every French schoolchild is expected to know, but which won't necessarily be known by people from other countries, even those that participated in some way in the events in question.

CÉSAR ET LA GUERRE DES GAULS

The Asterix cartoon books would appear to have some basis in fact. In 58 BC Julius Caesar followed his defeat of the Helvetians by pushing over the Alps into Gaul. In 57 BC he conquered the Belgians, followed by Brittany and Aquitaine. Having successfully crossed the Rhine, Caesar turned his attention to the remainder of Gaul. This remaining country was led by Vercingétorix, a feared warrior. All this corresponds broadly to the introduction of Asterix books which show that all of Gaul was conquered by the Romans with the exception of a small area led by a feisty chief.

The Roman army met that of Vercingétorix at Gergovie near what is now Clermont-Ferrand in June 52 BC and was soundly defeated thanks to Vercingétorix's brilliant tactics. Following this success, Vercingétorix was declared leader of all the Gallic tribes. He didn't stay leader for long because in October 52 BC his forces again met up with the Romans, this time at a place called Alésia. Everyone knows the name Alésia, but no one is now quite sure where it was. It is generally assumed to be somewhere in Burgundy. On this occasion Vercingétorix's army was completely encircled and, after a siege, Vercingétorix was taken prisoner. The remaining parts of Gaul were overwhelmed in 51 BC.

Caesar took Vercingétorix with him on his triumphal return to Rome in 46 BC, where Vercingétorix appears to have been strangled.

CLOVIS ET LE VASE DE SOISSONS

This is one of the great French legends. In 486, King Clovis I of the Franks, generally known as just Clovis, had been fighting the Romans under Syagrius and had just taken the town of Soissons. Pillaging by troops, especially of churches, was rife at this time and after the battle, Clovis's soldiers had stolen a particularly beautiful vase from a church. Learning of its theft, the bishop of Rheims sent a message to Clovis asking if the vase could be saved. When the king attended a sharing out of the booty he asked if he could have the vase to give back to the bishop. The assembled soldiers declared that all the booty belonged to their king and that Clovis could thus have whatever he wanted. However, before Clovis could take the vase, a soldier grabbed an axe and smashed it, crying that Clovis would only get what he deserved.

For some reason, Clovis did nothing at that time but, a year later, at a military parade, Clovis spotted the soldier again. He snatched the soldier's weapon and flung it on the ground. When the soldier bent down to pick it up, Clovis produced an axe and split the soldier's skull, crying, '*Ainsi as-tu fait au vase de Soissons!*' – that is what you did to the Soissons vase!

CHARLES MARTEL

Long before the Futuroscope was built nearby, the town of Poitiers was well known in France because of Charles Martel. In the eighth century the Muslim empire, having taken North Africa and Mesopotamia, moved into Spain – this explains all the Moorish architecture that can be seen there. Then, in 732 the Emir Abd er-Rahman, governor of Spain, invaded France in search of booty. Once he had sacked everything in Aquitaine, he set off with his mounted horsemen towards Tours, a town famed for its riches. At Poitiers he was met by Charles Martel and his army of Franks which was mainly made up of foot soldiers. Foot soldiers do not usually do well when faced with cavalry but Charles Martel was such a good tactician that he brought about a complete defeat of the invaders and the death of their leader. This victory left France free of the threat of invasion from the south.

What is interesting is that the Muslim horsemen were able to fight on horseback because they had stirrups, something that was unknown in France at that time. Three hundred years later the Normans would use stirrups to fight on horseback at the Battle of

Hastings, much to the consternation of the English, who had still never heard of them.

CHARLEMAGNE

All French schoolchildren know about Charlemagne because he did something absolutely unforgivable: he is believed to have invented schools. In fact, the story about his inventing, or at least visiting, a school was made up some seventy years after his death but this doesn't stop French children from believing it. They are supported in their belief by a well-known song by France Gall which includes the line, '*Qui a eu cette idée folle, un jour d'inventer l'école: c'est ce sacré Charlemagne*' – who had the mad idea of inventing school: it was good old Charlemagne. Whether he invented school or not – and who can doubt France Gall? – one could argue that Charlemagne should really be remembered for having improbably named parents: Pépin le Bref – Pepin the short, the son of Charles Martel – and Berthe au Grand Pied – big-footed Berthe. Perhaps inspired by his parents' odd names, Charlemagne went on to style himself *L'empereur à la barbe fleurie* – the emperor with a flowery beard. Nowadays we know him rather more prosaicly as Charles the Great who, as king of the Franks, created a massive Christian empire that covered much of western and central Europe.

1066

The battle of Hastings is one of the exceptions to the rule which states that battles are generally remembered more by the victors than by the losing side. In 1066 the Normans invaded England and changed the character of the country for ever. One might therefore imagine that the invading side would remember their success with pride, or at least mild satisfaction. In fact, French people hardly ever mention the Norman invasion; indeed, if you ask anyone about it they generally have only the haziest knowledge of who invaded whom and when.

The principal explanation lies in the nationality of the people who did the invading. They were not French but Norsemen. Normandy had been given by Charlemagne's successors to the Norsemen in order to make peace and so give the French a chance to recreate Charlemagne's old empire which had been divided and lost since his death. Thus, present-day French people don't believe that the invading forces had anything to do with them. The physical evidence has disappeared too: William of Normandy left from Dives but the port he sailed from has long since silted up and disappeared. The Bayeux tapestry – which is, of course, actually an embroidery – tells the story of the battle. However, it appears that French visitors to the museum are far less numerous than their British counterparts.

SAINT LOUIS

Everyone in France knows the story of Saint Louis – King Louis IX (1214–1270) – who dispensed justice under an oak tree in Vincennes near Paris. He apparently sat on a simple rug and dealt with all types of dispute, especially those involving poor people. This was particularly notable because justice had usually been dispensed by the feudal lords rather than by the king. Louis had helped Henry III of England retain Aquitaine and much of south-west France while renouncing his claim to the rest of the country. In return, Louis became king of this remaining, relatively small region of France. His reign is famed for being one of the more peaceful periods of French history.

JEANNE D'ARC

For years the only reply I could come up with to the common French accusation '*Vous avez brulé Jeanne d'Arc*' – the *vous* in question hopefully meaning the English generally and not me personally – was to ask the accuser exactly when it was that 'we' had burnt her. Nine times out of ten, they wouldn't know and the conversation could move on to happier topics. But what do you say to the tenth person, the one who knows that she was burnt on 30 May 1431? I have recently been given a splendid riposte to cover this situation: you ask where the English got the wood that was used to burn poor Joan. The answer will guarantee a brisk change of subject for it seems that the wood was happily sold to the English by local French people.

LOUIS XI

While Saint Louis is considered a good king and a nice chap, Louis XI (1423–1483) is remembered for being an effective king but an extremely unpleasant person. Judging by the portraits of him, he was also singularly unattractive. He was, however, a brilliant tactician. He managed to outwit Charles le Téméraire to reclaim Burgundy and Picardy which had been lost during the Hundred Years War. Louis then went on to acquire Anjou and Provence, thus recreating a sizeable kingdom. That he was not at all a nice person is shown by the fact that he is believed to have devised *les fillettes* – cages where prisoners were kept and which were carefully designed to be just too small to allow them to stand up or lie down fully.

HENRI IV

The first Bourbon king of France, ruling from 1589 to 1610, Henri IV is interesting for various reasons. He was the first Protestant king and, by the Edict of Nantes, he was able to give some political rights and religious freedom to the Huguenots. I like him for this as it appears that my ancestors were Huguenots who had to flee to England in the early sixteenth century. But more importantly, Henri IV seems to be one of the few kings in world history who managed to be upstaged by his own horse. There is a splendid equestrian statue of him – one of the first such statues to be erected in France – on the Pont Neuf in Paris. The one thing almost everybody knows about Henri is that his horse was white. About the only time Henri gets a mention nowadays is in a pointless non-question which you seem to hear remarkably often: '*De quelle couleur était le cheval blanc d'Henri IV?*' – what colour was Henri IV's white horse? It would seem that you have to be French to appreciate the point of it.

LOUIS XIV

The Sun King deserves a mention because, apart from all the extraordinary things he is known for, he is also notable for the rigorous organization of his day. It appears that every minute of his day, from the *petit lever* at 8.30 a.m. to *coucher* – going to bed – at 11.30 p.m., followed a strict timetable and, what's more, took place in the presence of a large number of courtiers. As he rose relatively late, his *déjeuner*, which was originally breakfast, was moved back to lunchtime. This created a need for a new word for his breakfast which came to be known as *le petit déjeuner*.

THE FRENCH REVOLUTION

As well as leading to a formal codification of the law, the French Revolution – which is, of course, just known as *la Révolution* in France – also brought about some surprising changes to the calendar. Thankfully, these changes didn't last as long as those made to civil and criminal law.

In 1792 a whole new calendar was devised comprising twelve months, each with thirty days. As this made 360 days, a further five additional days, known as *jours complémentaires*, were added at the end. The new calendar came into force on 22 September 1792 so the new revolutionary year ran from autumn to autumn. This explains the names chosen for the twelve new months: Vendémiaire (wine harvest); Brumaire (fog); Frimaire (frost); Nivôse (snow); Pluviôse (rain); Ventôse (wind); Germinal (germination); Floréal (blossom); Prairial (meadows); Messidor (harvest); Thermidor (heat); Fructidor (fruit).

Each month was divided into three ten-day weeks and each day consisted of ten decimal hours, each having a hundred minutes, in turn formed of a hundred seconds. A revolutionary minute was thus longer than a modern one, while the seconds were shorter than ours.

The days of the week were known as: Primdi, Duodi, Tridi, Quartidi, Quintidi, Sextidi, Septidi, Octidi, Nonidi and Decadi.

The new calendar lasted for twelve years, and was abandoned by Napoleon in year XII – or 1804. This move was extremely well received by the working people, who were delighted to go from having one day off in ten back to one day off in seven.

LA GRANDE ARMÉE

Somehow, calling it 'the big army' sounds more impressive in French than it would in English. This may be because of all the successes it brought Napoleon, or is possibly due to the fact that a smart Parisian avenue is named after it. In any case, the name is justified because it was indeed far larger than any previous army. It was created in 1805 by combining seven *corps d'armée*, each commanded by one of Napoleon's marshals, into a single entity. The corps d'armée were only combined at the time of a battle; the rest of the time they were separate entities which travelled independently. Each unit took its own route to their destination, making living off the land easier. They were never more than a day's march apart and were able to travel far more rapidly than the assembled army could have done. The strategy of separate groups travelling independently, then meeting up for a battle, proved itself at the battles of Austerlitz and Iena. The first Grande Armée was dissolved in 1807 but a second was created in 1811 which proved to be even larger, reaching 600,000 men at the beginning of the Russian campaign.

Sadly for those concerned, this Grande Armée didn't remain 'grande' for long. Forced to retreat from Moscow in 1812, French forces found themselves blocked by the Bérézina river. On 28 November, a fierce rearguard action took place while a bridge was thrown across the freezing water. Thanks to this, the majority of the troops managed to escape across the river but some fifty thousand died or were taken prisoner. The term *la bérézina* has since become a French synonym for defeat or disaster.

LES POILUS

A hundred years after the Grande Armée, France was forced to create a huge new army at the outbreak of the First World War. Of course, the war wasn't called that at the time, but was known as *la Grande Guerre*. The French soldiers who fought in the trenches came to be known as *les poilus* – the hairy men. The appalling conditions in the trenches were such that they were rarely able to shave and thus pictures show many of them with splendid luxuriant beards. Each year, remembrance ceremonies are attended by the handful of surviving poilus, who are now well over a hundred years old. Another term which dates from this period is *la Voie Sacrée*. This is a road which led from the town of Bar-le-Duc to the battle front at Verdun. For months in 1916 it formed the only route to the front for supplies and troops and thus played an important part in the final outcome of the battle. The modern road that follows the path of *la Voie Sacrée* is now numbered as RD 1916 in memory of the battle. Milestones still carry the name, *la Voie Sacrée*.

LA DEUXIÈME GUERRE MONDIALE

If you asked anyone in Britain what the dates of the Second World War were, they would more than likely reply that it started in 1939 and finished in 1945. Ask the same question in France and you will be surprised by a different answer: the war started in 1940. While Britain and France declared war on Germany in September 1939, the French didn't really get involved in anything until 1940 when Germany invaded France. This is reflected in a common French expression used when things really get going: *C'est parti comme en quarante* – it has started just like it did in 1940.

The French might also give a different answer to the question 'Where did the D-Day landings occur?' There were in fact two lots of *débarquements*, or landings, that the French have good cause to remember, given that they both took place in France. The first were obviously the landings in Normandy in June 1944. But two months later, in August 1944, there was *le débarquement de Provence* where a second allied invasion force landed with a view to forcing the Germans to fight on two fronts. This southern landing is interesting, first because many of the landing craft and barges used in Normandy were reused in Provence, but more importantly because a large proportion of the French army that landed under the command of De Lattre was made up of troops from France's then North African colonies. As is the way of things, the participation of the colonial countries was later overlooked or forgotten and soldiers who had taken part received smaller pensions than troops from France. France's later colonial troubles are often linked to the disillusionment that this produced and to the fact that the troops returned to their countries where they put their military training to good use in later conflicts with France.

10. Chasseur-cueilleur – how to be a hunter-gatherer

It is in the autumn that the French reveal their true colours.

Once the leaves begin to turn, French cities start to empty at the weekend. The city dwellers aren't leaving for their weekend houses, nor are they headed for the beach as it is far too cold. And, as it is too early for snow, they are not making their annual pilgrimage to the ski slopes.

In autumn, French city dwellers head for the forest in search of food.

In the UK you can find various books with titles such as *Food from the hedgerows* which explain to those not brought up in the country which edible plants can be found growing wild and waiting to be picked. Such books generally include handy recipes for nourishing and tasty salads and soups from things like wild sorrel or dandelions. I confess that, while I have leafed through various books of this sort, I have never felt the need to go foraging in ditches and hedges in search of strange-tasting foodstuffs, despite the fact that they are free.

Books of this type are far less common in France for the simple reason that the majority of French people have a very clear idea of what foods can be found for nothing in the countryside. This is mainly because France is far more rural than the UK. While many people in the UK come from families that have lived in an urban environment for several generations, a large proportion of French city dwellers are from families who moved from the country relatively recently. Thus, people who now live in towns and cities have parents or grandparents who still live in the country and who know about food for free and who have shared this knowledge

with their families. This may also explain the enduring popularity
of French markets.

LES CHÂTAIGNES

The foods that can be found in the countryside fall into two basic
categories: chestnuts and mushrooms.

When we first moved from Paris to a village lying near to a large
forest, our Parisian friends seemed to be keenest to come and see
us on autumn weekends. They would arrive, weighed down with
coats, gloves and stout boots, and immediately drag us off to
the forest brandishing carrier bags of assorted shapes and sizes.
'*Allez! On va chercher des châtaignes*,' they would cry, pushing us
before them. *Les châtaignes* are chestnuts, a food which is far
more popular in France than in the UK. In winter, Paris streets
are littered with chestnut sellers ladling out measures of roast
chestnuts from their braziers into paper bags. It is as well not to
look too closely during this operation as the measuring cup they
use is generally very grubby indeed.

But while bought roast chestnuts taste good, chestnuts that you
have found for yourself in a cold wood somewhere out in the
wilds taste far, far better. Or so the city dwellers seem to believe.

Some 40 per cent of France is covered with trees, most of them
deciduous. The deciduous woods and forests typically include a
fair proportion of *châtaigniers* – sweet chestnut trees. These are
not to be confused with horse chestnut trees – *marronniers* –
which produce the big, round, shiny chestnuts that are really only
good for playing conkers with. Sadly, no one plays the game in
France so all these wonderful conkers simply go to waste. I have

tried my best to interest French people in this fine tradition but it seems that the only thing harder than explaining the rules of cricket to a French person is trying to explain the point of a game of conkers.

Châtaignes are smaller, more oval-shaped and often come two or even three to a pod. Finding them is surprisingly easy as the tree does its best to advertise its position, littering the ground beneath it with vast numbers of empty husks and nuts. Once you have found your tree, all the chestnuts you want are there for the taking. Indeed, the quantities of chestnuts available in an average French forest are so large that if anyone else should come along and start picking up nuts under 'your' tree, you would probably just smile cheerfully and wish them well. There is more than enough for both of you.

Thus, an afternoon spent collecting chestnuts can usually be relied on to be an agreeable and rewarding experience.

The same is far from true of mushroom collecting in France.

LES CHAMPIGNONS

I have long believed that if you want a true insight into the French character, their real character, the one that you are generally not allowed to see in polite society, all you have to do is go and look for mushrooms in the forest.

Setting out for an afternoon's stroll with a view to *chercher des champignons* seems pretty much like a trip to find sweet chestnuts. The weather will be the same, the forest will be the same and you will wear the same clothes. The only visible difference lies in the stick. Arming yourself with a good stick – the sort of stick that, when stood upright, comes up to your chest – is a vital part of mushrooming. It doesn't have to be a professionally made walking stick: it is much better to find a good one on your way into the forest. It will mark you as a serious mushroom hunter. It also makes you walk more smartly, helping you stand upright as you stride boldly into the depths of the woods. The stick has two other useful functions: it is the tool that you will use to turn over the leaves in search of your prey; and it can be whooshed through the leaves to frighten off snakes. For the chances of encountering a snake during your afternoon stroll are much higher in France than in Britain.

Les couleuvres et les vipères

Experienced mushroom seekers have assured me that, when walking through the forest, you are most likely to encounter *une couleuvre* – a grass snake, a species which is not only harmless but known for being a lot quicker at getting out of your way than you are at getting out of its.

Unfortunately, you can also encounter various sorts of viper – *une vipère*. These should be watched out for as they are less good at fleeing than grass snakes and have only one way of showing their displeasure should you accidentally step on them: they bite you on the leg. If the experts are to be believed, being bitten on the leg or elsewhere is not life-threatening because vipers are sensible creatures and know that they have only a certain amount of venom available. What's more, they realize that what little venom they have should not be frittered away on passing, inedible legs, but used profitably on more edible prey. Thus, apparently, they bite you with enough venom to show that they are displeased, but don't waste their whole supply on you. This is all very well, but a bite from even a mildly displeased viper could well spoil your afternoon.

Spotting the difference between grass snakes and vipers seems trickier than might be thought because they can come in similar colours. The only sure-fire way is to look at their eyes, should you be willing to stay around long enough to do so. Grass snakes have round eyes while vipers have slit eyes. The fact that spotting snake eye characteristics in a gloomy autumn forest is a tricky thing to do accurately in the short time available explains why most people arm themselves with a good stick and why they spend much of their walking time dragging it noisily through the leaves.

'Où se trouvent les champignons?'

Now that we are fully equipped for an afternoon's mushrooming, we can confront the principal problem to be overcome: where do you find the mushrooms?

'Where do I go to find some nice mushrooms?' is a question that, sadly, seems to have no answer in France. In fact, it is not that it has no answer – it actually has a very good answer – but no one who knows is going to give it to you.

This is the first part of the true French character that I warned you about. A French person is genetically programmed to regard the location of edible fungi as a secret to be taken to the grave. Years of observation have convinced me that a typical French male would prefer to tell you his salary, the name of the candidate for whom he voted in the last election, or the name of his mistress, and possibly all three, rather than show you his favourite mush-rooming spot. The fact that no French male has ever told me any of the three will give you an idea of how unlikely it is to get him to tell you about the mushrooms.

Faire le loup

While no one will ever tell you where to look, everyone with whom you raise the subject of mushrooming will happily, even proudly, tell you that they know a really good spot. Not just a good spot, but a really, really great spot that is guaranteed to yield huge quantities of delicious mushrooms. Given the chance, they will then go on to boast about how they came to discover the spot in the first place. But don't bother asking where this fabulous spot actually is: the only reply you will get is a sucking in of air through the teeth accompanied by a regretful shake of the head. Few things are more irritating than this gesture. About the only thing that is more annoying is an alternative response to the question in which a long inhaled 'woooh' noise is made while tipping the head backwards. Jean, my first boss, called this gesture *faire le loup* – doing the wolf – because it sounds like a wolf baying at the moon. Jean also reckoned that the best way to get an elderly person to *faire le loup* was to ask them when they last had sex.

But you are probably thinking, 'How difficult can it be to find some mushrooms, for goodness' sake? You go into the forest and see where people are picking mushrooms, and then look there.'

This leads us to the second unfavourable aspect of the French character: they are really sneaky when it comes to hiding their favourite mushrooming spot.

We have seen the need to equip yourself with a stick and drag it through the leaves in order to drive away snakes. Unfortunately, it won't just be the snakes who hear you coming; other mushroom hunters, and more especially, mushroom finders, will hear you too. As soon as any such person hears you, they will move swiftly away from their spot and continue on a random, curved course, making it impossible for you to deduce where they were originally coming from. You will thus come across one or more smug-looking people, clearly identifiable as successful mushroom hunters, while having little chance of figuring out where it was that they found their booty.

Partager – to share, or possibly, not

The final, regrettable aspect of the French character will be revealed should you ever meet a French person after they have had a particularly successful afternoon's mushrooming. He or she will be staggering under the weight of a couple of large baskets, each filled to the brim with a selection of mushrooms. There will be far more than even an extended family of mushroom fanatics could eat in a week. Despite the fact that the quantities present exceed the limits of sufficiency and carry on well into the realms of excess, there is no chance whatsoever that the person will share them with anyone, especially you. This is true even if you know the person in question, and especially if you previously considered them to be a good friend.

La pharmacie

If, despite all the difficulties, you actually succeed in finding some mushrooms, a trip to the local chemist – may prove useful.

There are an awful lot of pharmacies in France: every village seems to have one. Our village of some five thousand inhabitants has two, both of which seem to thrive. Almost all the chemist shops in France are incredibly smart. For example, they all seem to have automatic doors which slide open noiselessly at your approach to welcome you into their opulent, hushed interior – for you will never hear a raised voice in a pharmacie. Once inside, it is immediately apparent that whatever you are going to buy is going to be very expensive indeed. But the calm and caring atmosphere coupled with the displays of beautifully packaged lotions, soaps and creams are so wonderful that you really don't care. And the *pharmacienne* in her immaculate white lab coat exudes so much knowledge and charm that whatever she recommends you will happily buy.

As well as selling expensive, beautifully displayed medicines and beauty products, a pharmacie is a good place to get information. Anyone who is in any doubt about exactly what sort of mushroom, or possibly, toadstool, they have found, will take it straight to the nearest pharmacie. There, assuming that it is the mushroom season, they will find clear and helpful posters showing the principal types of mushroom and how to recognize them, backed up with knowledgeable advice from the pharmacienne. The assistance on offer can go further than just help with mushrooms. If you know your pharmacienne quite well, or if she is a friendly sort, you can even turn to her for minor medical assistance – bandaging a cut, or getting something out of your eye.

COQUES, BIGORNEAUX, MOULES, ETC.

The only thing that seems to tempt the French into any semblance of purposeful activity on a beach is the thought of food. During the period of *les grandes marées*, or unusually high tides, the sea goes out far further than usual revealing great swathes of beach inaccessible for most of the rest of the year. (Of course, I am speaking about the Atlantic coast or the Channel here, not the Mediterranean.) As the time of low tide approaches, these stretches of sand are invaded by huge numbers of purposeful-looking people all armed with buckets and various sorts of digging implements. Most of them are looking for *coques* – cockles – which, judging by the speed at which the hunters fill their buckets, are just sitting there below the surface waiting to be collected. If you ask any successful cockle gatherer what they are planning to do with them all, they will generally launch into a mouth-watering description of the particular sort of mayonnaise that they are going to whip up when they get home and which goes especially well with cockles. Given half a chance, they will probably carry on and tell you which sort of wine is sitting in the fridge waiting to go with it.

If it isn't coques that they are looking for, it will probably be *moules* – mussels, *bigorneaux* – winkles, or even *couteaux* – razor shells. Really serious shellfish hunters arm themselves with a large and solid-looking version of a shrimping net which has the net mounted on a strong T-shaped frame. These aren't used for scooping things out of rock pools but for pushing along the beach. This leads to their common name of *pousseux*. When these nets are pushed along, a layer of sand is scraped into them. This is then sifted out, leaving any shellfish just sitting there waiting to be picked up.

LES HUÎTRES SAUVAGES

France's coastline is not made up entirely of beaches: there are rocky coves too. While not home to many cockles, these coves can be unexpectedly interesting places. I once spent a pleasantly aimless afternoon pottering on a deserted rocky beach near La Rochelle. I was vaguely looking for crabs and shrimps and so had been concentrating on the contents of the bigger rock pools and not the broad expanse of rocks nearer the sea. Looking up at one point I was confronted by the spectacle of an extremely pretty girl striding towards me. What was particularly striking was not the bikini she was wearing but the rugged-looking knife she was holding in her hand. For the briefest of moments I thought that my childhood dream of being James Bond confronted by Ursula Andress emerging from the waves had, against all probability, come true. But then I noticed that in her other hand she was clutching half a lemon. Surely, in the film, Ursula Andress hadn't been holding a lemon?

My dream was short lived for, with a complete absence of sideways glances, the girl strode straight past me towards the expanse of rocks. There, she squatted down and hacked at something on a rock with her knife. Having got whatever it was free she used a large stone to smash it, squeezed lemon juice on it and proceeded to eat it. When she moved on to start the hacking operation anew

I sidled discreetly nearer to see what she was doing. It was oysters – the rocks right by the sea were covered in them.

And there are all kinds of urban situations that you can use your hunter-gatherer skills in . . .

COMMENT CHOISIR SON FROMAGE

Even if you don't like cheese (if such a thing is possible) a *fromagerie* window is worth gazing at for a few minutes just to marvel at all the astonishing shapes, sizes and colours that are available. But if you go in to buy some cheese, you will quickly discover that you have to say a whole lot more than just, 'I'd like half a pound of that one, please.' If you are hoping to buy some goat's cheese for example, you'll have to be prepared to undergo a lengthy question-and-answer session before you are actually served. In reply to your request for something straightforward like, '*Un Crottin de Chavignol, s'il vous plaît*', you will be shown a wicker tray containing at least twenty of the things whereupon the question-and-answer session will begin. You will first be asked whether you like them hard or soft – '*plutôt sec ou plutôt frais*'. Once you have established that you like them soft, you should be prepared for at least two more questions about exactly how soft and how squishy you actually mean. Your replies to these questions will limit the selection from the original twenty down to a potential three. The salesperson's hand will now be hovering above the three in question but they won't be able to make a final choice until you have told them exactly when you want to eat it: lunchtime, tonight or sometime tomorrow. As soon as you reply '*ce soir*', their hand will fall, unerringly on a single cheese that fits all your requirements to the letter. You may not be able to tell the difference between it and any of its immediate neighbours, but the salesperson certainly can. And the cheese that has been selected will taste wonderful exactly at the moment that you said that you were going to eat it.

COMMENT CHOISIR SON MELON

One of the most entertaining pastimes, next time you find yourself in a French market, is to watch people trying to choose a good melon. There is a whole science to choosing a melon, an operation that is far more complicated than choosing any other fruit or vegetable. And just to make it especially interesting, some of the picking criteria carry more sexual innuendo than seems necessary for such a simple fruit. When faced with an array of melons, the first thing to look for is the number of darker lines spread around each one like lines of longitude on a globe. There should be ten of them. And the lines should be clearly defined. If you actually count the lines – which is probably not an occupation that you previously envisaged for yourself – you will find that there can be nine, ten or even eleven of them. Niners and elevens are to be discounted instantly because, as everyone knows, they don't taste as good as tenners (I have just devised these terms especially). The next thing to do is to ignore totally anyone nearby who advises you to pick male melons rather than female ones (or possibly vice versa). Despite strongly held beliefs to the contrary, melons don't have gender. Having dealt with the only objective, melon-choosing criteria, it is time to look at the subjective ones. First you have to examine the stalk. In most other situations, the stalk of a piece of fruit is called *la tige*. In the steamy world of melons, it is called *la queue* – which is also a slang word for the male appendage. The *queue* is surrounded by a pigmented circle called *l'auréole*, which, as you know, is also a word that applies to a part of the human anatomy. Those who don't want to get too involved with their melon will tell you just to pick a melon whose *queue* is ready to come off. However, true specialists think that pulling at melon stalks to see if they fall off in their hands is an inexact science. Such purists will start to sniff – *renifler* – parts of their melon. There are two schools of thought: the *renifler l'auréole* school, and the far more popular, but frankly obscene, *renifler la queue* school.

But what are you supposed to be sniffing for? It is a quite simple: *la queue* has to smell nicely of melon. What else?

11. Les enfants et les animaux — never work with small children or animals

LES ENFANTS

Talking to babies in any language is a risky business. Just pause for a moment to think of the rubbish you spoke when you were last confronted by an attractive baby. (Ugly babies are much easier to deal with because you don't usually speak to them at all.) I can't bring myself to write out the sort of thing that you are expected to say because it would look too awful in print, but I'm sure you know what I am talking about. Now imagine trying to say the same sort of thing in French. Yes, all of it – even the bits about tiny toes and little handies. Take my word for it: it is impossible.

There is, however, an easy solution to this problem: if you are faced with a French baby, why not chat to it in English? This may surprise the parents, especially if they don't understand what you are saying, but the baby won't care. The most important thing is that if you speak English, you can be fairly sure you won't make a complete fool of yourself.

Much harder than speaking to babies is speaking to toddlers. As toddlers are old enough to spot a foreign language, you can't cheat and speak English to them. You will have to speak French slowly and clearly while carefully picking the right words, assuming that somewhere along the line you have learnt the French for 'Is that your new teddy?' or 'What a nice fire engine – is it red?' In my experience it is incredibly hard to do. I always find that I end up sounding completely retarded, a fact which is quickly picked up on by the small child, who thereafter regards me with suspicion. I have spent ages thinking about this, but there doesn't appear to be a solution.

Nevertheless, in case you are ever asked to babysit a French child, or your children start playing with some French kids when you are next on holiday, a few typical words and expressions that are exclusive to children might come in handy.

Prems!

A perfect word to start with. A child who wants to stake his claim as the first to be allowed to have something, get the first go or receive the biggest piece will shout '*Prems!*' as soon as whatever it is has been offered. Unusually for a French word ending in 's', the 's' is pronounced so the word sounds just as it is written (though, of course, with a French 'rr' sound at the beginning). The child who isn't quite quick enough to shout first, but who is still quicker than the others, will grab second place by yelling '*Deux!*' This is pronounced as though it ends with a 'z' rather than with a silent 'x', presumably because it is a shortened form of *deuxième* – second.

Na!

French children are just as callous as any others and are quick to delight in someone else's misfortunes. If you announce bad news – there's none left; you are going to be smacked; I think you are smelly – you need a nice sneery sound to punctuate it and add a bit of insult to injury. Thus, having said whatever unpleasant thing seems appropriate at the time, a child will finish it off with a sharp '*Na!*' You can sometimes use '*Na!*' before the insult or even all by itself as a riposte to some unpleasant remark.

Another good sneery word is *Nananère*, which can be used in pretty much the same way as '*Na!*' As it is chanted rather than spoken, it has to end in an emphatic '*euh*' sound. It is used in much the same way as the British version, 'Na, na, na-na, na!' (or, possibly, 'ner, ner, ner-ner, ner!') This is also true of *Tralalère*, which is a victory chant to add to the end of some piece of news which is good for the child who is announcing it, but less so for the child who is hearing it.

Pouce!

If you have used '*Na!*' to good effect, you may well have so infuriated the other child that you find yourself being beaten up. Assuming that you are coming off worse, you will be keen to stop the squabble and negotiate some kind of settlement. Crying '*Arrête!*' – stop! – in an aggrieved voice won't bring things to an end because you haven't made clear the fact that you are calling a halt to the fight. You have to shout '*Pouce!*' – truce – (or, as we used to say, pax) in order to bring hostilities to an end. Children also refer to giving up or calling a ceasefire as *mettre les pouces* – sticking your thumbs up. If you are winning and are surprised that the other child hasn't given up yet, you can ask them whether they plan on doing so by saying, '*Pouce?*' in an interrogative tone.

On fait la paix?

Having brought hostilities to a close by calling *Pouce*, it is often necessary to agree to a long-term peace, 'long term' usually lasting no longer than until the next break time. Where, in my day, children said things like 'Be friends . . .?' in an ingratiating way, French kids opt for peace rather than friendship. Thus, one child, usually the one who has been coming off worse, will ask the other, '*On fait la paix?*' – shall we make peace? This has to be asked in a wheedling, ingratiating tone that is guaranteed to irritate the other child so much that they start trying to beat you up all over again.

'*C'est pas juste!*'

French children spend as much time as any others feeling aggrieved about something or other. When faced with an unwelcome instruction – it's time for bed; it's his turn now; you can't have any more ice-cream – they typically moan, '*C'est pas juste!*' – it isn't fair. Of course, it should be, '*Ce n'est pas juste*', but in such situations there is no time for grammatical niceties. In cartoon books, the expression is often written, '*C'est pô juste!*' where the *pô* sound reflects the moany, grumbling way in which it is said.

'*C'est même pas vrai*'

This is another expression which is used by dispirited children. Again, this should more correctly be, '*Ce n'est même pas vrai*' – it isn't true. A child who has been upset or put out by something said by another will go into denial by countering that whatever has just been said isn't true at all. Even when, quite demonstrably, it is. When saying, '*C'est même pas vrai*', all the emphasis has to go on the word *même*. Frowning heavily while saying it is also important.

The same sort of principle applies to another expression, '*Même pas mal*'. This is the cry of a child who has just been smacked or hurt in some way. Just to show how tough he or she is, the kid will claim, '*Même pas mal*' – it didn't hurt at all – usually just before bursting into tears.

'*Bébé Cadum*'

If they see you burst into tears, your French comrades will really have no choice but to ridicule you for crying so easily. Chances are they will show exactly how pathetic they think you are by calling you *Bébé Cadum*. This comes from a long-standing and very well-known advertising campaign for Cadum soap – a famous French brand – based on an apparently adorable baby who has just been washed with Cadum soap. Obviously, it is never flattering to be compared to a cute, clean baby. As the other kids really want it to sting, they chant, '*Oh … le … Bébé Cadum!*' – just like a derogatory football chant.

'*Zizi*'

When we were sniffing melons in the previous chapter we saw that *queue* is a slang term for the male appendage. *Zizi* is another word for the same thing but is principally used by children. It is a bit ambiguous because some children, and even some adults, use it to refer to girls' bits as well as boys'. Others, who prefer to have one word for one thing and another word for something quite different, use *zizi* for boys and *zezette* when referring to little girls. All this makes you wonder what the dancer Renée Jeanmaire's family was thinking of when they let her change her name to Zizi.

'Caca boudin'

The two elements of things lavatorial are *pipi* and *caca*. *Boudin* is a derogatory word for an ugly girl as well as referring to black pudding. Small children wanting to swear without using any of the more grown-up words stick the words *caca* and *boudin* together to make the all-purpose insult, *caca boudin*. For best effect you have to curl your top lip in a sneer while saying it.

Childhood instincts are never really forgotten. We have a friend who, while driving through our village did something so daft that it made a man coming the other way hoot, gesture and insult her thoroughly. When it was her turn to reply, words failed her. All she could manage by way of riposte was to dredge up a memory from the playground and shout, '*Caca boudin!*' This apparently was so devastatingly unexpected that the man stalled his car in shock.

Des jeux

Some French children's games to end on:

Chat

This is the French version of 'tig', or whatever you used to call the game where one child is 'it' and has to chase after the other children. This is presumably a reference to *jouer au chat et à la souris* – to play cat and mouse. The child who is 'it' is *le chat*. Sometimes there is a special place where you can't be caught. This place is called *la maison*. If you want to claim sanctuary and avoid being caught, you have to touch it and cry, '*maison!*'

La marelle

The game of hopscotch is just as common in France as it is in Britain, possibly more so. It is known as *la marelle*, a name which is also used for a strategic board game where two players place counters on an array of points.

1, 2, 3, soleil

British kids play, or, very possibly, played, a game called 'What's the time, Mr Wolf?' French kids play *1, 2, 3, soleil!* One child faces a wall while all the other children stand some distance away. The child facing the wall repeatedly calls out, '*1, 2, 3, soleil!*' while the others move closer. On the word *soleil* the wall-facing child turns round and tries to spot anyone who is not completely immobile. Anyone seen moving is out. The winner is the first to touch the wall or the child.

Plouf, ploufer

If you are going to play *chat* or *1, 2, 3, soleil!* you are going to have to choose someone to be 'it'. Saying, 'Eeny, meeny . . .' won't get you far. You have to go *Plouf* to find out who it is going to be. The verb for picking 'it' is *ploufer*, a made-up verb based on the fact that when you point to each child in turn you go, '*plouf, plouf, plouf!*' You generally start off with a rhyme or song, pointing to each child in time with the words, finally saying, '*plouf, plouf, plouf!*' at the end. The last *plouf* selects the child. Some children put the *plouf* business before the rhyme.

LES ANIMAUX

And then there are animals. People who like animals generally sound as gormless when they speak to them as fond parents cooing to small babies. If you really want to have a go at chatting to an animal in French, the first thing to know is that you can't just translate 'Hello, pussy' or 'Hello, dog'. '*Bonjour, minou*' or '*Bonjour, chien*' doesn't work because without the definite article it doesn't make any sense. Thus, you should say, '*Bonjour, le minou*' or '*Bonjour, le chien*' when meeting the animal for the first time. This principle can be used with any sort of animal as you will see if you ever take small French children to the zoo.

Les toutous

When speaking to dogs French people seem to be far more flattering and encouraging than they are when speaking to people. A good opening gambit, to get the dog on your side, is to compliment it by saying, '*Il est beau, le chien*' – what a nice dog – or, more endearingly, '*Qu'il est beau, le chien-chien.*' If you want to use the equivalent of 'doggy', you could say, '*Il est beau, le toutou.*' You can also encourage it not to bite you by telling it how kind it is: '*Il est gentil, le chien*', or, again, *le toutou*. To have any chance of being given a paw you will have to ask, '*Tu donnes la patte?*' or, possibly, *la pa-patte*. If after this you are getting on sufficiently well to start throwing a ball for the dog to fetch, you should cry, '*Va chercher la ba-balle!*' while throwing it. 'A ball' is normally *une balle* but to a dog it is a ball-y and is thus referred to as *la ba-balle*.

Similarly, if you want the dog to go and look for a bone you should say, 'Va chercher le no-nos!' – no-nos is used instead of os for a dog's bone. Repeating the first syllable like this seems to be a key feature of talking to French animals. And if ever you find yourself faced with a particularly elderly dog, one with lots of white whiskers, you should call it Pépère, encouraging it to follow you, for example, by saying 'Viens, pépère.' When talking to people, Pépère means 'granddad'.

The large number of dogs in Paris has led to an excellent invention: la caninette, a cross between a motorcycle and a carpet shampooer. These machines cruise the streets of Paris and, when one comes to a mess left by a dog, the rider stops beside it, lowers a mechanical arm with a spray nozzle and a vacuum cleaner head, and whooshes the mess away. If you watch the rider's face during this process, you will see that it usually has the expression of one engrossed in a dangerous, and extremely delicate operation, one on which lives may well depend.

Le Yorkshire

Before we leave the subject of dogs, one particular breed deserves a special mention. Le Yorkshire – the Yorkshire terrier – has its own special place in French society as it is clearly the dog of choice for numerous French ladies of a certain age. It is increasingly common in Métros and trains to spot the head of a Yorkshire poking out of the top of a designer bag clutched by a doting owner. Indeed, once outside the home, the dogs seem to spend their lives being carried. The advantages for the owner are considerable: they get a friendly companion who can be endlessly dressed up with ribbons and little coats, the dog doesn't cost much to feed and doesn't need to be trained to come when called because it never leaves its mistress's side. It is easy to pamper because French dog food manufacturers even produce special, expensive food just for *les Yorkshire*. From the dog's point of view, the advantages are more dubious. Can it be worth putting up with all this pampering, not to mention the indignity of being called 'Jimmy' or 'Kevin', just so you don't have to walk too far?

Les minous

There seem to be fewer phrases used when talking to cats than there are for dogs, probably because you are not as likely to encourage a cat to fetch a ball-y or give you its paw. But once you have mastered the principle of *le chat* or *le minou* you can make up suitable expressions like, '*Il est beau, le chat*', or, even, '*C'est qui, le beau chat?*' – who's a nice cat, then? – or, possibly, '*C'est un joli chat, ça*', said in a flattering, positive tone of voice. If you want to call a cat – and this is as likely to be as successful as it would be if you called it in English – you have to shout, '*Minou, minou, minou . . .*' rapidly in a high-pitched, ingratiating tone.

There is an excellent cat-stroking word in French. It describes that stroking under the chin thing people do to cats that makes them stretch their necks out and go 'soup faced', as we used to call it. It is known as *papouille*. It is usually used by cat-loving women who start stroking your cat and then pretend to be the cat speaking, saying, '*Ah des papouilles! Que j'aime ça.*' Being a French, cat-related word, there are probably sexual overtones in there somewhere. And then there is *chatte*, a word that is way, way beyond sexual overtones. It is, ostensibly, the word for a female cat but its more common meaning is something else entirely. The odd thing about it is that it is most often used by mature women who have a female cat at home and will insist on telling you about the ways that they have been playing with it. I can never believe that these women don't realize the enormity of what they are saying. Surely they must be doing it deliberately.

12. Les boissons – the essentials of drinking

Driving south one day, a pressing need for coffee caused us to stop in a village lost somewhere in deepest rural France. There is still quite a lot of rural France about and some of it is very rural indeed. This village only had one café and the urge for coffee was so strong that we went straight in, despite the fact that it had 'PMU' on a sign outside. PMU stands for Pari Mutuel Urbain and it generally means that the café is home to horse-racing enthusiasts who use it to place their bets and watch the races on a TV screen. Being Sunday morning, there were no races and the TV was switched off so we sat down at the table under the screen. Barely had we started on our coffee and croissants when the barman called out, '*Ça commence*' – it's starting – and turned on the TV above our heads. At this, all the customers – who were all male and all quite as rural as the village – moved closer to the screen, forming a semicircle around us.

The programme was the weekly horse-racing news show. Unfortunately, rather than just a discussion about racing, there was a special report on racehorse breeding. We thus found ourselves surrounded by blue-overall-wearing blokes with ruddy faces and flat caps who spent long minutes leering lewdly at a series of pairs of racehorses who were energetically and very noisily doing their best to make baby racehorses just above our heads.

This is definitely not conducive to relaxed, Sunday-morning conversation. It is therefore as well to check carefully before you walk into a café or a bar in France.

UN BAR OU UN CAFÉ?

Telling the difference between a café and a bar is surprisingly difficult. The only formal definition lies in the fact that they both need to have something called a *Licence IV* in order to be able to trade. This is a licence dating from the Second World War which is enacted by a law known as the *Loi du 24 septembre 1941*. The text of this is displayed by law on the wall of any café or bar and states:

Autorisation de vendre les boissons des 1er, 2ème, 3ème et 4èmes groupes: rhums, tafias, alcool de vins, cidres, poirés, liqueurs anisées édulcorées de sucre ou glucose et autres liqueurs édulcorées ainsi que du 5ème groupe: toutes boissons non interdites.

The summary at the end – *toutes boissons non interdites* – means that the establishment is free to sell anything that is not *interdit*, or banned. The only banned drink that I know of in France was – until 1988 – absinthe. Thus, if you are looking for anything but absinthe to drink, you should find it in a café. Or even in a bar.

The practical difference between bars and cafés really is hard to pin down. It seems to be a matter of what the owner supposes that you are going to do in the establishment. If you are expected to sit down at a table and have a leisurely cup of coffee, the place will probably be known as a café. If, on the other hand, the proprietor has envisaged customers standing at the bar or perched there on a tall bar stool while they have a beer or a glass of red wine, it is likely to be called a bar.

In fact, the difference is not that important because you can order a drink in a café or a coffee in a bar. Also, you can generally order sandwiches and snacks in both cafés and bars.

'C'EST MA TOURNÉE!'

If two or more people go into a British pub together, the quickest, or the most generous, will react first and offer to buy a round. As soon as one of the others has finished their drink, they are obliged by the system to cry, 'My round', or 'Same again?' or whatever and buy a new set of drinks. The principal effect of this system is to make sure that people who go to pubs spend most of their time there drinking. While people pay for others' drinks in France, there is not the same urgency to get a new round in as in Britain. The French view of going to a bar could be summarized as, 'We go there to have a chat while we are having a drink' whereas in Britain it would seem to be more a case of, 'We go to the pub to have several drinks, and chat too if possible.' 'My round' in French is 'C'est ma tournée', but this isn't heard that often, mainly because you order the drinks from the waiter and don't need to get up and go to the bar.

LES BOISSONS

Some drinks are typically French and seem particularly suited to being drunk on the terrace of a café when on holiday.

Non-alcoholic drinks that are refreshing after a hot day's sightseeing include *un citron pressé* – freshly squeezed lemon juice with a bit of granulated sugar to make it drinkable; *un diabolo menthe* – a shot of mint cordial mixed into a glass of lemonade; *un Perrier menthe* – a similar shot of mint cordial mixed into a glass of Perrier; *un Vittel menthe* – the non-fizzy version of Perrier menthe.

There are also alcoholic drinks that are equally refreshing such as *un panaché* – beer and lemonade; *un Monaco* – un panaché to which has been added a shot of grenadine cordial to make it taste different and give it a red colour; *une mauresque* – pastis to which has been added a shot of barley water. Adding shots of various cordials to things seems to be a recurring theme of French drinking culture.

Absinthe

You may remember that, until recently, the only thing you couldn't drink in a French bar was absinthe. But what was so terrible about it that a Licence IV specifically used to ban it?

Absinthe is a strongly alcoholic drink made from anise and wormwood – *Artemisia absinthium*, hence absinthe. The ingredients also include fennel and the herb hyssop. The drink is green in colour but turns milky, like pastis, when you add water. Adding water is a good idea because absinthe is incredibly strong – up to 72 per cent alcohol. It was known as *la fée verte* – the green fairy – because of the magic spells it cast over you when you drank it. As it is so bitter, you have to add sugar as well as water before drinking it. Adding the sugar became so much a part of the drinking ritual that special ornate spoons were made just for this.

The hallucinations and madness that are always attributed to drinking absinthe – Van Gogh's mental decline was blamed on his excessive consumption of the drink – and which led to its being banned, come from a combination of the high alcohol content and the presence of thujone, the active ingredient of wormwood, which is believed to be a mild hallucinogenic. The ban on absinthe dates from 1915 but has been lifted because it is now believed that you can drink well-made absinthe in moderation without suffering the infamous side effects.

UN TOAST!

You have made it! You are now sitting comfortably, in convivial company, somewhere in France with a full glass in your hand. Life is great! But before you can taste your drink, someone has to propose a toast.

If you are with someone special, you could opt for something simple but personal, like '*Á toi*' as you raise your glass to him or her. If circumstances permit, you could perhaps change this to, '*Á nous*' – to us – or, even, '*Á nos amours*'.

A single friend can be toasted with a simple, '*Á ta santé*', while to someone you know less well you could say, '*Á la vôtre*'.

If you are with a group of friends, you can toast them collectively by saying, '*Á nos amis*', while guests can thank their hosts with '*Á nos hôtes*'.

Interestingly, and confusingly, *un hôte* can mean both a host and a guest, as I found out when someone insisted on paying for me, saying, '*Vous êtes mon hôte*'. I couldn't make any sense of this because I thought it meant, 'You are my host', in which case, why was he paying?

ET GLOU, ET GLOU ET GLOU ...

Once you have finished the toasts and had a drink or two, you may well feel the urge to do some singing.

Here is the classic French drinking song. You won't need to know any others.

The point of this song is to get you to touch your full glass successively to your forehead (*le front*), your nose (*le nez*) and your chin (*le menton*) before knocking the drink back in one. In the song, for reasons that may never become clear, the words *front*, *nez* and *menton* have been transformed into fake Latin words and thus become *frontibus*, *nasibus* and *mentibus*, possibly because it makes the song scan better. It goes like this:

> *Ami Dédé, Ami Dédé*
> *Prends donc ton verre*
> *Et surtout, ne le renverse pas*
> *(Attention André, attention hein!)*
> *Et porte-le du frontibus au nasibus au mentibus*
> *Et glou, et glou, et glou, et glou, et glou, et glou ...*
> *(Bravo!)*
> *Il est des nô-ôtres*
> *Il a bu son verre comme les au-autres*

Key things to know are:

- Dédé is a familiar form of André in the way that Nick is a shortened form of Nicholas.
- As you are singing in a loud, tuneless and bleary way the phrase *Il est*

des nôtres – he is one of us – is dragged out and becomes *nô-ôtres*. In fact, it generally comes out as *nô-ô-ôtres* and is usually sung louder than the rest of the song.

- And, most importantly, the gulping sound – it might be written in English as 'gulp, gulp' or 'glug, glug' – as you knock back a drink is '*Et glou, et glou, et glou* . . .' in French. This is what you sing while the victim, who is the one doing the forehead-, nose- and chin-touching with his glass, drinks it down in one to general acclaim.

So gather some friends, open a bottle and get singing. The fact that you don't know the tune is of no importance whatsoever.

HOW TO GET THE RIGHT CUP
OF COFFEE

It is time to have a cup of coffee to sober up a bit. But what sort of coffee should you order?

Un café

Ordering *un café* in a French café or bar will get you one thing only: a small cup (and saucer) of strong black coffee known as *un express*. *Un express* – a term you can also use to order the thing in question – is defined as being coffee made by forcing hot water under pressure through coffee grounds.

Un café noisette

If the idea of a large cup of milky coffee doesn't appeal to you, but you don't fancy drinking your coffee black, you could try *un café noisette*. This is an express with a small amount of milk added to it. It will come in a usual express-sized cup, but will be fuller than a cup of black coffee. You thus get the feeling that you have had more for your money and have the taste of milk too. It generally costs a little more than an express but a lot less than a *café crème*. A *noisette*, as it is often called, can be ordered after a meal, as well as in the morning, without incurring the same disdainful look from the waiter that you get if you order a *café au lait* after a meal. *Noisette* actually means hazelnut, which is just what this neat little cup of coffee looks like with its crown of light brown froth.

Un double express

This is exactly what the name suggests – a double shot of strong black coffee served in a bigger than usual cup. It is generally ordered early in the morning by weary-looking people who have clearly had a tougher time than usual getting out of bed.

Un café long, court, serré

Merely because you just fancy a plain black coffee doesn't mean that you can't personalize it in some way. Rather than simply call for *un café* you can go on and specify exactly how you would like it without being perceived as fussy or annoying. If you want the cup filled to the brim with coffee that is slightly (such things are relative) weaker than normal, you can ask for *Un café long, s'il vous plaît*. More probably, if you are French, used to strong coffee and in need of a fix, you will call for your coffee *court*, or even *serré*. *Court* is more concentrated than normal and the cup will be less full, while *serré* will get you something close to Italian coffee in which the spoon will tend to stand up.

Un café et un verre d'eau

This is one of the more useful suggestions that you will find in these pages. When you take a break from your sightseeing for a well-deserved and reviving cup of coffee, try asking for a glass of water with it. People tend to make this a sub-order, separate from the basic request for a coffee. You hear someone say, '*Un café s'il vous plaît*'. Once the waiter has acknowledged the order, the customer might add, as though having only just thought of it, '*Avec un verre d'eau*'.

You'll only get tap water, generally out of a spigot located somewhere near the beer taps, but it will be free and you will find the combination of coffee and water surprisingly refreshing.

'Ah-ha!' I can imagine you are thinking, 'He has forgotten *café au lait*!'

Actually, he hasn't, but you will have to wait till Chapter 15 to read about it. And it may turn out to be something of a disappointment.

HOW NOT TO PAY TOO MUCH FOR YOUR DRINKS

My first boss, who knew a thing or two about Parisian cafés and bars, used to take me for a beer now and again in his beloved François Premier bar. That my boss was a really good customer was first shown by the fact that my initial interview for the job with him took place in the bar rather than in the company's offices. It quickly became clear that he was a regular customer as he knew the barman by his first name, Yves, and treated him most politely despite what seemed to me to be his unpleasantly surly air. Yves wore a grimy black apron with a series of pockets on the front for storing different coins, had greasy hair and a distinctly shifty look about him. He invariably added up the bill to his advantage but he also had a special way of getting even more money out of his hapless customers. To each bill Yves ostensibly added an extra franc (this was many years ago) to the total, claiming that this was a present from the customer '*pour mon fils*' – for my son. What's more, the franc for his son was added to the bill whether the customer wanted it to be or not. No one apparently knew whether the son ever received any or all of the money.

Hardened sceptics in the François Premier were heard to wonder darkly if he actually had a son at all.

In a British pub you order your drinks at the bar, then either drink them standing up at the bar or take them to a table and sit down. In either case, the price of your drink is the same whether you stand or sit inside or even if you go outside into the garden.

Differences can occasionally arise between prices in different bars of a given pub.

In France, and most especially in Paris, the price of a given drink is a function of the part of the café in which you choose to enjoy it. The cheapest place to have a drink – or *consommation* as it says on the menu card fixed, by law, to the wall of any café – is at the bar itself. The bar is often known as *le zinc* in view of the fact that bars used to be topped with a sheet of zinc metal. Sadly, bars with real zinc tops are increasingly rare and synthetic materials are nearly everywhere. Alternatively, you can choose to sit down, inside the bar, and wait to be served. The fact that French people are used to being served sitting at a café table explains the bemused look you can spot on the faces of French tourists who wait in vain to be served at tables in British pubs. If ever you see such tourists, please take pity on them and explain that, in order not to die of thirst, they should go and buy their drinks at the bar. If you decide to have coffee sitting down at a table in a Parisian bar, the price increases but the coffee remains the same.

Then there is a final possibility, for those of an extravagant nature, which is to have your coffee outside at a table on the terrace.

At a terrace outside one of the smarter cafés in the Champs Elysées, on the sunny side of the street, the price of any drink, even a simple cup of coffee, can reach heights you would not have imagined possible. Imagine a typical scene: it's a sunny lunchtime in Paris, and a group of amiable but inexperienced tourists stop at Fouquets for a reviving beer each. Fouquets – oddly enough, the 't' at the end is pronounced just as it would be in English; whatever you do, please don't try to say 'Foukays' – is probably the most famous and therefore most expensive bar along the Champs Elysées. And it isn't even on the sunny side of the avenue. Four decent-sized beers at a table outside Fouquets cost as much as a reasonable meal in an English restaurant. The routine is always the same. Having drunk their beer, the luckless tourists call for the bill. It arrives – a simple scrap of white paper folded over and placed on a red plastic saucer. One of the tourists unfolds it. A long moment of puzzlement follows. He looks around him, perhaps beset by thoughts of candid cameras. He turns the bill over and looks on the back. He looks at other tables in case he has got someone else's bill by mistake, but there is no respite forthcoming. He passes the bill to his friends, muttering nervously, 'Hey, you guys, have you seen this?' They can see it, but they don't believe it. One of them translates the amount into their own currency. 'Fifty bucks for four lousy beers!'

I smile cruelly and walk on.

I must confess that this is an activity which never palls, even after all these years, and I wholeheartedly recommend it to you. The important thing is to make sure you play the part of the spectator and not the payer.

13. Les restaurants – a guide to eating out in France

One of my first business trips, shortly after starting work in France, was to Pau. Not wanting to return empty-handed, I had stopped on the way to the airport to buy several tins of *confit de canard* as well as a few bottles of Madiran – the local, strong red wine. Arriving at Orly, I staggered out of the airport, clutching my carrier bags, to find a long queue for the taxis. I put the bags and my briefcase on the ground and nudged them forwards each time the queue moved a little. With each movement, the plastic bags clinked and chinked cheerfully. 'That sounds interesting!' said the man behind me. 'What have you got there?' When I explained about the confit de canard he got extremely animated. 'Yes, but how are you going to heat it up?' Confit de canard is already cooked before being put in the tin, and only requires heating rather than further cooking.

Naive and foolish, I said that I was probably going to heat it up in a frying pan. This, I quickly realized, was not the right answer at all.

'Heat it up in a frying pan?! *Ça va pas?!* You heat it up by putting it in a preheated oven for ten minutes.'

At this, the woman in front of me in the queue turned round and added, 'Yes, but you really must put it skin side upwards, otherwise it'll be all soggy.'

This was too much for the couple ahead of her. 'Skin side upward, of course, but no one in their right minds puts it in a preheated oven. In our family, we always put it in a cold oven, turn on the heat, and when the oven gets up to 200 degrees, the duck is ready. That way, you heat it through gradually.'

A long and excited discussion ensued between the various

participants, all of whom, except me, had extremely strong views on the matter. Some spoke of grilling the duck to get crispy skin (I must say that I quite liked the sound of that). Other queue members within earshot occasionally chipped in with views on accompanying vegetables (potatoes fried in the duck fat from the confit tin was the only view on which practically everyone agreed); wine (thankfully, the Madiran seemed to have been the right choice); and suitable desserts to finish off with. All this lasted in great good spirit until my turn came for a taxi. For all I know, they carried on talking about it long after I had gone.

Food is definitely not something to be treated lightly in France, whether in a restaurant or at home.

HOW TO DECIPHER A RESTAURANT MENU

À volonté

If you are hungry or on a budget or, especially, if you are hungry *and* on a budget, this is a term to watch out for. For *à volonté* means 'as much as you like'. Of course, not everything on the menu will be offered *à volonté*. It will typically only be *frites* in a steakhouse or *mousse au chocolat* for pudding. If you opt for French fries *à volonté*, it really does mean what it says. If you finish all the ones you were originally given, you can ask for more and a new side plate of fries will arrive. The only minor problem will be trying to catch the waiter's eye in order to ask for some. It is simpler with puddings such as chocolate mousse because generally what happens is that the waiter brings a serving bowl of the stuff to your table and leaves you to get on with it. Both of these examples are particularly desirable if you are in the company of hungry adolescent offspring (please excuse the tautology).

Arrivage, selon arrivage

Arrivage refers to something that has come in, whether to the local fish market straight from the sea, or to the fruit and vegetable market. The term is most commonly applied to fish and is used either to let you know that the sole or red mullet may not be available because none has been caught today, or as a vague way of saying, 'You can have whatever it is that we found this morning at the local market.' Whatever it actually turns out to be, at least you can assume that it will be fresh.

En vedette

Une vedette is a star. Thus, a dish *en vedette* should be thought of as a somewhat special dish of the day. It is usually shown up on a board together with its price. Alternatively, where there are several dishes of the day, it will probably be the one the restaurant is most proud of. It is often a good dish to pick if you can't make your mind up between several possible candidates.

Price rule

If you have decided not to have one of the *formules* that are on offer but plan on choosing your meal *à la carte*, you may want to try to get an idea of what you will end up paying at the end of the meal in order to avoid any unwelcome surprises. Rather than going carefully through the menu adding up the price of each of the various dishes that you are thinking of having, a rough and ready rule of thumb is to take the price of the main course and multiply it by three. The result will be roughly what you pay for a starter, main course, dessert and some reasonable wine.

Vin/boisson compris

This is a good thing to look out for: some menus or *formules* include drinks. Generally you are given a choice between red or white house wine, usually 25 cc in a glass carafe or an earthenware jug, bottled beer or a bottle of mineral water.

À la ficelle

In some brasseries they won't serve you anything less than a bottle of wine but assure you that they sell it *à la ficelle*. When you tell them that you have no idea what they are talking about, and that you don't want a whole bottle thanks very much, they point to a chart on the wall. This has the silhouette of a wine bottle, drawn life-sized, with graduations down the side. They bring you a full bottle and, when you have finished your meal and call for the bill, they take your depleted bottle over to the chart, measure the level left, and read off the price on the scale. It works really well. The only disadvantage is that having a nice bottle of wine sitting on the table makes you extremely likely to drink more than you had originally planned. This can work out quite expensive. It is also not clear what happens to whatever wine is left in the bottle when you leave. And once you are sitting down . . .

Le cocktail maison

If you don't fancy a kir, but don't really know what you feel like drinking, you can always opt for one of these if it is on offer. *Le cocktail maison* usually comes in two forms – alcoholic and non-alcoholic. Either way, it is generally rather brightly coloured, sometimes even carefully poured to create bands of different coloured liquids. It may even be festooned with some kind of swizzle stick. As the content, not to mention the vivid colour, of such drinks varies considerably from restaurant to restaurant, it is a good idea to ask for more details. The waiter will generally be delighted to tell you what their particular cocktail maison comprises and may even, if you think it is important, describe the colours for you.

Petits fours salés

If you do decide to order an apéritif – and, frankly, why wouldn't you? – you can expect to get something to nibble with it. The least you can expect are some peanuts or a small bowl of olives. If it is a restaurant specializing in fish dishes you may well get a small dish of *crevettes grises* – small shrimps. Alternatively, if you have chosen a North African restaurant in search of couscous, your drinks will most likely be accompanied by a small plate of spicy vegetables that you eat with a cocktail stick. All these nibbly bits are known as *petits fours salés* or even *petits trucs salés*. However, do be sure to speak very clearly – so you don't end up chewing sadly on *un petit salé* which is a chunk of salt pork.

LE MENU

The majority of *entrées* and *plats* that you will find on a French restaurant menu will most likely be well known to you. Choosing between the various dishes on offer is simply a matter of taste because they are generally all delicious. Rather than list the more common, perfectly appetizing dishes, I thought it would be more useful to mention a few that might prove less tempting should you happen to order them inadvertently.

How to avoid the more unpleasant dishes

You have to draw the line somewhere. However much you adore French food there are a few dishes that must be viewed as going beyond acceptable limits. I have included an explanation of one or two of the worst offenders so that you can either avoid them like the plague or, if you are made of sterner stuff than I am, actively seek them out.

Andouillette

If you look up a definition of *andouillette* in a cookery book, you will probably discover that it is a small *andouille*. More specifically, it is said to be a small andouille that is served cooked. If that's the only explanation you get, you can count yourself very lucky because you could have stumbled across an alternative definition which reads, 'A length of a pig's large intestine, stuffed with lengths of its small intestine'. If you are still with us and haven't fallen to the floor in a swoon, you will be able to appreciate my mother's consternation when, having ordered andouillette by mistake, she saw the offending object placed in front of her. To her credit, while she didn't actually eat any of it, she did spend a considerable time spreading it artistically around her plate, thus creating the illusion that she actually had eaten quite a lot of it.

Boudin noir

A *boudin* is a pudding and is also, as we have seen, an unflattering term that is applied to a girl who is not quite as thin or as pretty as she might be. *Un boudin noir* is the French version of black pudding, and thus, probably the least awful of the dishes listed here.

Boudin blanc

This is positively appetizing compared to some of the dishes here. *Un boudin blanc* is a length of intestine filled with a mixture formed of chopped up chicken and milk.

Cervelles

I'm starting to regret making this list! There are two words for 'brain' in French. There is *un cerveau*, which refers to the brain while it is in the body, whether human or animal. Then, there is *cervelles* which refers to the corresponding bit of an animal, generally lamb, once it has been cooked. Another dish to avoid, perhaps?

Ris de veau

I have always viewed this as a particularly sneaky and deceitful dish. This is because, when I first saw it on a menu at one of the first lunches I had with my colleagues in Paris, I didn't spot that it said *ris* with an 's' rather than *riz* with a 'z', which I knew meant rice. Thus, I foolishly believed that I was ordering veal with rice. Given that I didn't understand any of the other dishes on offer, this struck me as a fairly safe bet. Unfortunately, what turned up in front of me was not 'veal with rice' but something I now know to be called sweetbreads. This, I'm prepared to admit, is an odd choice of name too as there is no bread, nor anything sweet involved in the dish whatsoever. For those who aren't familiar with the term 'sweetbreads' – and lucky you if you aren't – it has something extremely unpleasant to do with a pancreas.

Tripes à la mode de Caen

If you look up the French definition of *les tripes*, you get *viscères comestibles d'animaux*. This, as you may have guessed, means 'edible animal viscera'. Tripe, whether *à la mode de Caen* or elsewhere, is an acquired taste in France. Many people hate it. Those who love tripe talk about it all the time and tend to be members of tripe clubs that meet once or twice a year for tasting and cheery discussions of a tripe-related nature. *Tripes à la mode de Caen*, if by any chance you haven't jumped to the next chapter, is a recipe using four different sorts of animal stomach. The recipe also calls for onions, carrots, salt and pepper, white wine, bouquet garni and brandy.

It sounds as though it would be really tasty if they just left out the tripe.

Things that don't necessarily appeal at first or second sight

Foie gras

The only problem with foie gras is that, once you understand how it is made, you can't really justify eating it, or, at least, knowing how it is made helps you to come up with all sorts of justifications for not eating it.

Unfortunately, there is another equally strong problem: foie gras is absolutely delicious.

Escargots

While I can understand why people eat foie gras, I have never really seen the point of eating snails. This is mainly because they are generally served with a strong garlic butter sauce so you really just get the texture of the snails and not their taste. However, without the garlic, it is not clear what, if anything, a snail would actually taste of. So why not eat something nicer with garlic sauce on it? Another reason to hesitate before ordering snails is that some restaurants apparently shamelessly create their own 'snails' by refilling used snail shells with chunks of something else. The something else is reputed to be bits of animal lung.

Frogs' legs

For once I can aspire to the moral high ground here as I have never eaten a frog's leg. This is mainly because I once saw a documentary that explained the harvesting process. Also, people who have tasted them say they taste like chicken. In that case, perhaps it would be simpler to eat chicken?

But let us leave such sensitive subjects and have a look at one of the true wonders of France.

LE FROMAGE

Everyone knows of General de Gaulle's cry of despair as he wondered how anyone could govern a country that has at least three hundred sorts of cheese.

As far as I'm concerned, anything that can alarm Le Grand Charles simply by existing peaceably in large numbers deserves a special mention here.

The fundamental thing about cheese in France is that it is eaten before dessert and not afterwards as it is in the UK. French people believe, and there is much to support their point of view, that a meal should end on a sweet note rather than on a cheesy one.

Lovers of oatcakes or cream crackers as supporting media for a piece of cheese should be warned to avoid French cheese courses for fear of disappointment: such things are never eaten in France. The only accompaniment for cheese that is considered acceptable is bread (and, of course, wine). Or nothing at all if you are feeling really full. If you are not using bread, you are expected to eat your cheese neatly with a knife and fork.

Plateau de fromages

When looking at a menu, and anticipating the arrival of the cheese course, it is important to know that there is a difference between the terms *un fromage* and *plateau de fromages*. If the menu refers to *fromage* in the singular, then that is probably what you will get

– a single piece of cheese served on a plate. *Fromages* in the plural may get you the same plate but with two or three pieces of different sorts of cheese on it. What is really worth looking forward to is when it says *plateau de fromages*. This should mean that a trolley, or at least a decent-sized tray, festooned with different sorts of cheeses, will be brought to the table for you to choose from. However big the selection, though, you are going to have to be really charming, or really lucky, to be served more than three different pieces.

Rather than discuss the classic cheeses that you are all familiar with, I just want to mention two favourites that are worth looking out for: one for its taste, the other for its name.

Boulette d'Avesnes

When the cheese trolley arrives next time you have a decent meal in a French restaurant, look closely and, if you are lucky, you may spot, lurking near the back, a *boulette d'Avesnes*. It is easy to recognize as it is one of the few pyramidal ones, and certainly the only reddish one. It is generally the one hiding near the back, trying to look innocent. It may very probably be the only one on the trolley which hasn't had a slice cut out of it. There is a good reason for this, for we are dealing with the Surprise Symphony of French cheeses: despite its innocent appearance, it tastes stronger and spicier than almost any other cheese, or, at least, than any other cheese that hasn't gone completely off. It is actually delicious, once you have got used to it, especially if you wash it down with a glass of strong dark beer, preferably one from the north of France, where the boulette comes from.

Coup de Pied au Cul

The attraction of this particular cheese lies more in its name than in its taste. *Coup de pied au cul* means 'a kick in the arse'. It was the brainchild of a cunning Norman cheese maker who developed the cheese in Calvados in 1951 and hit upon the name that would ensure its success both in France and abroad.

The cheese is claimed to have a distinctive taste because a key element of the manufacturing process involves sloshing neat Calvados (the potent apple brandy that is native to Normandy) over the outside before leaving it to *affiner* in a cellar for two and a half months. I am prepared to believe this because, as far as I can see, if you sloshed neat Calvados over pretty much any foodstuff, I'm sure it would taste fairly memorable after being left in a cellar in Normandy for two and a half months.

'Comment est votre Camembert aujourd'hui?'

Proof that cheese is a subject of vital importance in France, should such proof be necessary, can be provided by my old colleague Gaby's cheese ritual. Every day, when we used to go to the restaurant together, he would call Claudie the waitress over to our table as soon as he had finished his main course. In the tones of one asking a question of paramount importance, he would enquire, '*Comment est votre Camembert aujourd'hui?*' – how's the Camembert today? He was not enquiring after its health, but its suitability for his fastidious consumption. Camembert quality is a variable thing: its colour, texture, flavour and, of course, smell can change as a function of its age as well as depending on how and where it has been stored. Claudie would always reply to

Gaby's question with great seriousness and honesty. The Camembert, according to the day, might be perfect, slightly doubtful, not really worth bothering with or to be avoided at all costs. If there was the slightest doubt about its suitability, Claudie would bring the cheese to Gaby for inspection. This involved a fair amount of study, sniffing and even poking before Gaby reached his decision. If Claudie said something along the lines of, '*Monsieur, franchement, je ne vous le conseille pas, aujourd'hui*' – I really can't recommend it today – Gaby would forego his cheese and sulk for the rest of the afternoon.

Incidentally, Gaby always ate his Camembert by cutting it into wedges and adding a knob of butter, a practice that I copied and still follow to this day.

AND THE POTENTIAL SIDE EFFECTS OF ALL THIS FOOD ...

If you are going to eat in France, you will have to be prepared to get in touch with your digestion. For the French are very aware of theirs. One of the hardest things to understand when I first encountered French people was their frequent references to their digestive systems and, more specifically, to something called *une crise de foie*. When you try to get someone to explain what this actually is, they tend to translate it literally and claim to be suffering from 'a liver crisis'. At first sight a liver crisis sounds terribly dramatic and you find yourself wondering how the person suffering from it is still bravely there in front of you rather than in intensive care. Further questioning over several encounters with unfortunates stricken by liver crises leads you to a more jaundiced view of their problems. For *une crise de foie* turns out to be nothing more than an upset tummy resulting from having over-indulged in rich food or alcohol or, generally, both. It has very little to do with the liver at all. Nevertheless, you will occasionally spot seasoned liver crisis sufferers throwing themselves upon the content of mysterious bottles with labels such as *Hépatoum*. The names of such para-medicines give support to the sufferer's view that their symptoms are connected with the liver. But don't let that fool you: it's really just glorified indigestion. In my more cynical or, possibly, realistic moments I start to believe that there is a certain psychological element to *crises de foie*. Several notable sufferers seem to be laid low by such crises when they have been upset by something or even rendered jealous by something lucky happening to someone else. I had a colleague who, when jealous or *contrarié* – upset – by something, would sink into a deep sulk while claiming that he was in the throes of a *crise de foie*. His secretary, a charming motherly sort, generously described him as being *très sensible du foie* – having a very delicate liver.

But references to things digestive are not limited to crises de foie. The terms *digestion* or *digérer* come up in conversation alarmingly often in France. Of course, it would be wrong to say that it comes up in 'polite' conversation because the subject of one's digestion is not considered a suitable one by certain people in France. Those who do mention it, and they are numerous, will be heard to say of some foodstuff, '*Je ne peux pas le digérer.*' This clearly translates as 'I cannot digest it.' But what do they really mean? As far as I can make out such people simply mean that eating whatever it is gives them indigestion or makes them burp a lot. What is highly entertaining is trying to explain to French people that the British rarely mention their digestion at all.

Claiming that the nearest English expression for 'I cannot digest red peppers', for example, is to mumble, 'I like red peppers but they don't like me', meets with blank incomprehension.

14. Le serveur –
how to deal with waiters
and find the loo

You are in a restaurant, the main course has just been cleared away, you have had a glass or two of wine and life is looking pretty good indeed. The waiter returns to your table to discuss the question of puddings. If you decide to have a pudding and ask what sort of thing is on offer, you may well find yourself the victim of a French waiter's favourite form of torture – listing the puddings to a foreign visitor.

Your intellectual faculties will not be at their best at this point: it is not necessarily the moment you would have picked for any sort of brain-teaser. Unfortunately, the waiter knows this too and will thus take malicious pleasure in listing all the puddings at great speed, typically starting with *les tartes*. It starts innocently enough. '*Nous avons de très bonnes tartes*' – we have some very good tarts – he says, to get your attention. Poor innocent that you are, you will fall head-first into the trap by asking what sort. With a smile he will reply,

'*Nous avons tarteauxpommestarteauxquetchestartetatintarteà-laframboise . . .*'

However good your French, you will not be able to understand a single word of this high-speed list. Seeing you reeling open-mouthed from this first salvo, the waiter will press his advantage by swiftly moving on to the sorbets and ice-creams: '*Nous avons aussi des glaces.*' This time he won't wait for you to ask what sort, he will merely carry straight on:

'*Nous avons glaceàlavanilleglaceauchocolatsorbetaucitronsor-betaucassis . . .*'

You won't understand a word of this either and will thus suffer the humiliation of admitting defeat by asking him to repeat his lists slowly and clearly.

Even when they are not torturing customers, waiters have their own particular vocabulary.

'SOUHAITEZ-VOUS PRENDRE UN APÉRITIF?'

One of the first things you will hear a waiter say is, '*Souhaitez-vous prendre un apéritif?*' or, possibly, '*. . . un petit apéritif?*' Some people, in reply to this enquiry, order the bottle of wine that they are going to drink with their meal, thinking that the first glass will play the part of their apéritif. This is all well and good, but there is a trap to avoid if you do this. If you reply, 'Non . . .' in response to the waiter's question and then go on to order your wine, you will get the bottle of wine but no nibbly bits will arrive with it. It is vitally important to say, 'Oui . . .' before saying that what you want is actually a bottle of wine. That way you should get the olives or nuts or whatever the restaurant generally serves with proper apéritifs, as well as your bottle of wine. This occasionally works even if you just decide to have mineral water as your apéritif.

'CHAUD DEVANT!'

This is certainly not something that you will hear in a smart restaurant. Rather, it is the cry of a busy, hurrying waiter in a cheap and cheerful brasserie. Anyone carrying a hot plate or dish somewhere will use this cry to warn people in their path that they are bearing down on them and that if they were planning on getting out of the way, this might be a good time to do so. It roughly translates as, 'You there in front of me! – this is hot!' Friends carrying serving dishes to the table, whether hot or not, cry, '*Chaud devant!*' and I have even heard removal men, their arms full of boxes, use it to clear a passage for themselves through a crowd.

'J'ARRIVE!'

At some point in the meal, you may want to call the waiter to your table. A good way to do this is to cry, '*S'il vous plaît?*' in an interrogative tone. In response to your cheery '*S'il vous plaît?*' there is a fair chance that the waiter will smile and reply, '*J'arrive!*' in a bright, reassuring manner. *J'arrive!* translates quite simply as 'Coming!' In any reasonable circumstance you would expect someone who calls 'Coming!' to approach your table fairly soon after assuring you that this is what they are going to do. Unfortunately, the important thing about *J'arrive!* is that it can only ever be pronounced by a waiter who, at the time, is walking at considerable speed in a direction exactly opposite the one that would lead to your table. It would be wrong and unjust to assume that the waiter has no intention of coming to find out what it is that you want. It is simply that circumstances prevent him from doing so at that particular moment. By crying *J'arrive!* he wants you to understand that he really will come over as soon as he has finished whatever it is he is doing, assuming he doesn't forget or find something more interesting to do in the meantime. It is, however, probably safe to assume that he really will turn up eventually.

'ÇA A ÉTÉ?'

The first time the waiter comes to clear away your plates, for example after the first course of your meal, he will be wanting to check that all is well and that you enjoyed whatever it was that you just ate. Instead of asking something complicated such, '*Est-ce que cela vous a plu?*' – did you enjoy it? – he will often just say, '*Ça a été?*' in an encouraging, interrogative tone. This roughly translates as, 'Was it OK?' Of course, this sort of informality will only be heard in mid-range restaurants. The more chic the restaurant, the more formal the waiter. Because the question is short and informal you are not expected to reply with an extended eulogy about your salad or an in-depth analysis of the herbs and spices used in the sauce. A simple '*Très bien, merci*' will suffice. Of course, if the question is actually longer and more formal it may deserve a more enthusiastic reply, such as '*C'était vraiment délicieux*', assuming, of course, that it was.

Either way, there is a fair chance that the waiter won't actually listen to your reply as he will be busy clearing the plates.

'J'AI VU QUE MONSIEUR AVAIT BEAUCOUP APPRÉCIÉ'

Sometimes my enthusiasm for good food gets the better of me. In a little restaurant in Saint-Martin-de-Ré I had the best chocolate dessert in my life to date. It was so delicious, so perfect, that it would be unfair to try to describe it to you here. Suffice it to say that it was pretty amazing. And very chocolatey. Being so good, I really enjoyed eating it and may possibly have made more enthusiastic noises about it than are usually considered acceptable in Île de Ré restaurants. It is also possible that, trying to get the very last scrap, I may have appeared to try to climb into the bowl. Either way, when the waiter came to clear away the bowls, I turned my chocolate-smeared, beaming face up to him and tried to convey how good it had been. At this, he turned to Inès with a slight, sardonic smile and said, '*Je me suis permis de regarder et j'ai vu que Monsieur avait beaucoup apprécié*,' – I took the liberty of looking and I noticed that Monsieur enjoyed it very much. While this sounds very polite, it was in fact a wonderful example of withering, waiter-ish sarcasm.

HUSTLING

When business is slack, some waiters step outside the restaurant to accost passers-by and try to drum up trade. This is particularly common in certain touristy streets in Paris that have a series of similar restaurants, but the practice can also be spotted in some seaside resorts. For years I completely missed the point of being hustled. A waiter outside a restaurant would encourage us to come in and my instinctive reaction was to walk briskly on with a firm *Non, merci*, congratulating myself on not having been pushed into accepting a restaurant that I hadn't chosen. Only recently did I discover that it is far more profitable to stop and ask the hustler why you should choose their particular restaurant over all the others in the street. Whatever the answer, you must then claim emphatically that another hustler down the road has just said exactly the same thing, and that you are thinking of going back to that restaurant because it looked very nice. Don't worry if your French isn't up to all this because the hustler's English will be more than adequate – otherwise they wouldn't have been chosen for the post.

You have now entered a negotiation phase where the hustler, who really doesn't want to see you turn round and head back to the competition, is going to have to start making some kind of concession to tempt you to stay. The most likely ploy will be to offer you a free *apéro* with your meal, usually making it clear whether this means a *kir* or possibly a *cocktail maison* of some sort. This may well be enough to make you think, 'What the heck?' and let yourself be led inside. If it isn't enough to sway you, and you enjoy a bit of tough bargaining, you may well be able, if you insist long enough, to get a free coffee thrown in at the end as well.

LE SOMMELIER

If the restaurant is extremely smart, you will also get *le sommelier*. This is the wine waiter, whose job, as the name suggests, is to help you choose the wine to drink with your meal. He, for it is almost always a he, will also bring the wine for you to taste and stay to share the moment when you actually taste it. However, in some outrageously smart restaurants, the sommelier actually does the tasting on your behalf. He comes to the table with the bottle that you have ordered, shows it to you to gain your approval, and then goes off with it to a nearby wine trolley. There, he opens it and tastes it all by himself, either in a glass or in one of those silver tasting cups known as *un tastevin*. If he is satisfied, he returns somewhat smugly to the table, tells you how wonderful it is and starts pouring it. I find this irritating: not only are you not allowed to approve your own wine but, more annoyingly, the sommelier always seems to taste far too much of it and staggers back to the table with a much-depleted wine bottle and a smug grin.

The most important thing about wine tasting is that you do it to make sure the wine is fit to drink. Things do go wrong between the moment the wine is in the fine oak barrel (or in the large stainless-steel tank, depending on what sort of wine you have ordered) and the moment it is poured into your glass. Everyone, including the sommelier or the waiter, knows this: that is why they ask you to taste it just to be sure all is well. Everyone agrees that there is a finite possibility that the wine that you are going to taste has something wrong with it.

A simple rule may be of help here: if it tastes like wine, it is probably OK. If it tastes horrible and your first thought is to spit it as far away as possible, then it has gone off. And you should have no qualms about saying so to the waiter. If he doesn't believe you, he is free to pour some into another glass and have a taste himself. Waiters quite often do this and you shouldn't take it to mean that he doesn't think you know what you are talking about.

The only real problem is what to do if you think that the replacement bottle tastes just like the first.

LES TOILETTES, AND HOW TO
FIND THEM

At some point during a meal in a restaurant, the need may arise to visit *les toilettes*. Before we consider possible phrases that you can use to ask the waiter how best to find them, it might be a good idea to be warned as to what may await you when you get there.

If we assume for the moment that you have actually managed to find the place you seek, your difficulties aren't necessarily over when you get there. For, when you push open the loo door there is a high probability that you will find the room in darkness. This is something I have noticed sufficiently often to generalize about it here. The lavatory light, which generally has the weakest bulb in the building, is always turned off when you get there. This has always struck me as peculiar because the saving of electricity must be really small, whereas the difficulty created for the visitor is considerable. You have managed, often not without difficulty, to identify the right door of the place you are looking for and you push it open to find you can't see anything. So you set out to feel around for the light switch, often fumbling around on the walls or optimistically groping for a string pull. A word of advice: never waste your time looking for string pulls in France – they haven't been invented yet.

You may be lucky and find a simple light switch which will usually be of ridiculously flimsy construction and which will emit a pathetic 'ping' as you switch it rather than a good, solid 'click'. But what you are more likely to find is a time switch of a sort that you have never seen before. These seem to come in two types: ones that you have to push hard, or ones that need to be twisted firmly in order to obtain light for a given length of time. If you guess that it is the sort that needs to be pushed, you can be sure that it is one you should have twisted. And vice versa. But at last you have managed to turn the light on and are free to get on with whatever it was that you are there for. Unfortunately, your difficulties still aren't over. The time switch, as we have seen, is intended to keep the light on for a predetermined length of time. This time is carefully calculated to be exactly eight seconds shorter than the time you need to complete your mission. Thus you will find yourself unexpectedly, and most inconveniently, flung into complete darkness at a time when you would have actually preferred to be concentrating on something else entirely. You therefore have to abandon whatever it was you were doing and start fumbling around the walls again to relocate the accursed light switch.

When all is over and you are preparing to head back to your table, you may possibly, and quite understandably, feel that you really ought to enter into the spirit of the thing and turn the light back off as you leave, assuming the switch lets you do so, simply to make sure that the next poor person undergoes the same, character-forming experience as you have.

And how should you ask your way to the loo? In my experience, the best way is to start by setting off purposefully from your table in a direction more or less chosen at random. While you are walking, you will either bump into a waiter or catch someone's eye. In either case you can just say, 'Les toilettes, s'il vous plaît?' in an interrogative tone. Of course, if you have just caught the eye of a member of the restaurant's staff, you don't even have to say the words out loud. They will easily understand from seeing you wandering around the restaurant, and your mouthed enquiry, what it is you are looking for.

Having judged the calibre of the person they are dealing with, the member of staff will probably make their reply by way of some helpful gestures rather than a long-winded explanation of how to find the place you seek.

Le savon

Despite the annoyance of finding the loo light off, your visit to *les toilettes* may well include a positive note because of the soap. For you may be lucky enough to stumble on one of the few surviving places in France that still use that strange bar of soap which is fixed to the wall. Instead of having an ordinary bar of soap left on the side of the washbasin, which might fall victim to desperate soap thieves, the soap is mounted on the wall above the sink on a bracket in the shape of a swan's neck. Generally oval in shape, and a dark yellow colour, the soap looks a bit like a large, ancient lemon. What's more, it is free to rotate about the arm of the bracket. When you want to wash your hands, you first make them wet and then rub them round the bar of soap while it rotates in an interesting, slithery way on its bracket. Unfortunately, washing like this concentrates your efforts exclusively on the palms of your hands because you can't easily rub the soap on the backs. Another snag with this arrangement is that you can't easily rinse the soap under the tap before or after use and so you generally arrive to be confronted with a dark, grimy lump that quite puts you off using it. Nevertheless, it is worth making the effort to find it, and then rinse it as best you can, because it is far more memorable than these newfangled liquid soap dispensers which you now see everywhere.

15. Les étrangers — how not to look like a tourist

On one of my first ever trips to the restaurant to have lunch with my new colleagues, we all ordered various sorts of steak – steak, entrecôte, bavette and whatever.

When the food was ready, the waiter breezed cheerfully up to our table carrying a couple of plates. He looked down to check what they were and, having done so, cried, '*C'est qui, l'anglais?*' Being the only English person present I was thrown into confusion. How did he know that I was English? I hadn't heard anyone tell him. And anyway, why would they? Could it be that he had done something terrible to my meal as revenge for some historical or sporting event that had upset him? Or was it something to do with my bad French or my ridiculous accent?

All these questions raced through my mind while I gazed helplessly at the waiter. Despite all my doubts, my inner courage (or my hopeless stupidity) got the better of me and I raised a tentative finger in the manner of one answering a question asked by a particularly fierce schoolteacher and said, '*C'est moi l'anglais.*'

For a simple declarative sentence, these few words produced spectacular results. The waiter stared at me as though he had just noticed that I had two heads and sneered, '*Hein?*' in disbelief, while my new colleagues all exploded into mocking laughter. Calming them down seemed to take several minutes. Finally, one of them recovered enough to explain that the waiter hadn't actually said *anglais* but *onglet*. *Un onglet* is a prime cut of beef.

This is an extreme example of how to make it patently clear to all those around you that you are not French.

There are a whole lot of other things that, if you are not careful, will lead to your being spotted as a tourist the minute you get to France.

Just ordering a cup of coffee can be enough.

UN CAFÉ AU LAIT ...

All these years you may have been going to France and asking for '*un café au lait, s'il vous plaît*'. And why not? You have always got what you wanted so what could possibly be wrong? Nothing really – apart from the fact that, in Paris and much of the rest of France, people only seem to use café au lait for the stuff you make at breakfast time in your own home. If a French person's breakfast is to involve coffee and milk it will very probably also involve the presence of an oversized, cheerfully coloured bowl. Into this bowl is poured a measure of coffee according to taste and a quantity of milk. The milk in question will quite possibly be hot and very probably sterilized. The resulting mix of coffee and hot milk in a bowl is the only one that can truly be called a *café au lait*.

It is, however, extremely unlikely that you will ever be served this sort of bowl of milky coffee in a café or a bar. That is why ordering a *café au lait* marks you as a tourist in the eyes of everyone within earshot.

So what, then, should you order? Simple: '*Un café crème, s'il vous plaît*', despite the fact that no cream of any sort will be involved in making it. You can even refine your order so as to appear as French as possible by simply saying, '*Un crème, s'il vous plaît.*' Better still, in many cafés they offer two sizes of *crème* which means that you can call for *un petit crème* or *un grand crème*, according to your mood.

TREMPER SA TARTINE

But even if you correctly order your coffee you may still find yourself the subject of a cold, calculating stare from the nearest French person simply if you are not seen to do something when you have coffee at breakfast. To find out what, you just need to sit a French person at a table on which is placed a bowl of *café au lait*, and stick a *tartine* of bread, butter and jam in their hand. In such a situation, they are genetically programmed to do one thing: dunk the tartine in the coffee – *tremper sa tartine dans le café*.

Not dunking your tartine in your coffee won't necessarily give you away as a tourist. However, if you do dunk it – and, if you do, you will be very glad you did – you considerably increase the chances of the gaze of any watching French person sliding coolly over you and on to someone else.

Incidentally, the French expression for dunking a biscuit – *tremper son biscuit* – has an alternative, extremely rude meaning. I know: I have single-handedly silenced a smart tea party by using it.

Other, seemingly innocent actions will also mark you as a tourist.

POTATOES

For example, how should you pronounce the word 'potatoes'?

Increasing numbers of fast-food restaurants offer tasty segments of potato as an alternative to conventional chips or French fries.

These are known on the menu as 'potatoes'. But how does a native English speaker, particularly one who is trying not to draw attention to themselves, pronounce this? Should you pronounce it the English way, despite the fact that it will be in the middle of your order, the rest of which you will be doing your best to pronounce with your sophisticated French accent? If you do, there is a good chance that the person serving won't understand and will make you repeat the only word that you are sure of having pronounced correctly: '*Un double burger, un grand coca et des quoi?*' To this, you will have to meekly try to say the word 'potatoes' in a mock French accent, despite the pain it causes you, in order to get your message across. The only alternative is to go for this strategy from the outset, reassuring yourself that, anyway, you are trying to say 'burger' in a French accent, so why not go the whole hog and order some 'pottattows' too?

Of course, 'potatoes' won't be the only English word that you may have to pronounce in the course of a French sentence: all sorts of other words have slipped into the French vocabulary, despite all the efforts of the Académie Française. Words like 'brownies', 'coleslaw' and 'smoothie' are now commonplace. They are all amazingly tricky to pronounce for a non-French person, especially, in my experience, 'brownies'. Whether you order one or sixteen of the things, the 's' at the end is pronounced. Thus, you can call for, '*Un brownies, s'il vous plaît.*'

COMMENT METTRE LA TABLE?

One of the easiest giveaways that mark you as being non-French is the way you deal with knives and forks. There are two potential pitfalls: when you lay the table, and when you put your knife and fork down while you are eating. You can quite easily tell whether a table has been laid by a British person or a French person: you just have to look at the forks. British people lay the forks with the point uppermost while on a French table the forks are placed points downwards. Apparently, it has something to do with family coats of arms, which, historically, were on the back of French forks and on the front in Britain.

Of course, you probably won't be going to lay anyone's table while you are on holiday but, should the occasion ever arise, it is good to be able to avoid the traps.

Even if you manage to lay the table properly, you may still get caught out in the middle of the meal when you put your knife and fork down for a moment. While in Britain people tend to put their knife and fork down in a 'twenty past eight' position, with their tips crossing somewhere near the middle of the plate, many French people opt for the *ailes de mouette* – seagull wings – strategy. This involves laying the knife and fork in a position closer to 'quarter past nine' than 'twenty past eight', with the handles resting on the table and only the tips resting on the edge of the plate. But, as ever, there are those who frown on this strategy, believing it to be socially unacceptable. Indeed, some people don't so much frown as scowl when faced with a knife and fork that spill off the plate in an indecorous fashion. Whether such people are right or not to scowl and frown at other people's cutlery, it won't really concern you as there is no particular reason why a visit to France should inspire you to adopt the *ailes de mouette* strategy, seeing as you don't do it at home. You will thus, even without knowing it, be spared the unpleasant experience of being harshly judged by people you don't know.

Given that you have probably never worried about how to put down your knife and fork when eating abroad, you have perhaps been hurriedly giving the matter some thought and are now wondering whether the French have some sneaky, special way of leaving their knives and forks at the end of the meal.

Well, they do.

Like many British people, I was always taught to leave my knife and fork parallel to each other on the plate at the 'half past six' position. French etiquette also says that the knife and fork should be left parallel to each other. There is, however, a disagreement about the correct time. In France, the accepted time for leaving your knife and fork is at the 'twenty past four' position, that is, at a slight, but artistic angle towards the right.

DE LA CONFITURE

We have seen what traps cutlery may hold for the unwary in France. Other, completely innocent-looking things may also cause you to blow your cover and be spotted for being British. One of these is jam.

It is breakfast time and you are having some toast and jam, or, possibly, marmalade. You take a spoonful of jam (or marmalade) from the pot and then either dump it on your toast or, if you are being polite, put it on your plate. Either way, the spoon will be used only for the operation of getting the jam out of the pot. For the next stage, that of spreading the stuff on your toast, you will put down the spoon and pick up a knife. Of course you will: that's what you have always done. Unfortunately, the minute you start spreading jam on your bread with a knife, you run the risk of feeling the hand of the French secret police on your shoulder and hearing a chilling '*Venez avec nous*' – come with us.

It was the knife that gave you away. The majority of French people will never use a knife but will use the spoon both to get the jam out of the pot *and* to spread it on the bread. Why they do this is not clear: a spoon is not the optimum tool for jam-spreading. You only have to look at someone spreading jam with a spoon and you will see that they have to spend ages making fastidious, circular movements to get the jam evenly spread. Conversely, with a knife, in a couple of sweeps the job is done. What's more, using the spoon in this way increases the chances of getting butter into the jam pot. This is something that never happens if you opt for the spoon and knife combination.

LA POLITESSE À TABLE

Having dealt with one or two things that it is perhaps better not to do when eating in France, it might now be useful to consider something that you shouldn't say if you are invited for a meal.

Your hosts will have gone to a lot of trouble to get the meal ready for you. You will hopefully manage to show your appreciation for all their efforts by not saying *Bon appétit* before tucking in. Some people believe that this expression is common, but the principal reason why you are *not* supposed to wish someone *Bon appétit* is that it reflects badly on the quality of the food on offer. If you think about it, it is not very flattering for the cook or your host if your first reaction on seeing a dish arrive on the table is to think, 'Well, I hope you're feeling really hungry today, because from the look of *that*, it's the only reason you are going to eat it' and sum all this up by saying, '*Bon appétit*'.

Even if you have avoided this pitfall at the beginning of the meal, there is still a risk that you will go and spoil it all at the end.

Your hosts knew you were coming so, obviously, they will have prepared enough of everything so that you can have as much as you want. This should really go without saying so there is no need for you to say anything in French that corresponds to 'I am full' when you finally get to the end. You have just had a brilliantly prepared meal in generous quantities. While you are not necessarily expected to have gorged yourself to a state where you are physically incapable of eating another mouthful, you should at least be assumed to be gastronomically sated. There is thus no reason to say anything apart from a pleasurable '*Merci*' at the end of the meal.

And the one thing you *really* shouldn't do is try to translate 'I am full' directly into French. The result is guaranteed to be disastrous. At first sight, the translation seems so easy: you obviously know the French for 'I am' – *je suis* – and 'full' was one of the words you learnt at school – *plein*. Stick them together and you get *je suis plein*. You may even remember enough school French to be able to say *je suis plein* if you are male, and *je suis pleine* if you are female. Whatever can be wrong with that?

It is probably worse for women. *Pleine* is a term that is applied, quite correctly, to animals to show that they are in the happy state of expecting progeny. It is never used for women. A woman expecting a baby is *enceinte*, never *pleine*. Thus, if you try to say 'I am full' you will unfortunately end up by inadvertently claiming that you are heavy with calf. This will not necessarily be good for your image. If a man says, '*Je suis plein*', people will not assume that he misguidedly believes that he is going to have a litter of piglets; however, they may assume that he is admitting to being drunk. *Plein* can be a synonym for *ivre* – drunk – though many people believe that the word can't be used on its own but has to be used as part of a compound expression: you have to be as *plein* as something. You could thus describe yourself as being *plein comme un huître* – as full as an oyster – an expression that means being really drunk.

Whether *plein* means drunk or not, it should be clear that your life will be a lot happier if you manage to refrain from using it at the end of a meal.

16. L'ennemi héréditaire – how the British are seen in France

What do the two following French expressions have in common?

- *L'ennemi héréditaire*
- *Notre meilleur ennemi*

They both, as I am sure you guessed, refer to the English. For the French have a somewhat particular relationship with their neighbours across the Channel.

But this relationship is a complex one. People often ask me why the French hate the English so much. The simple answer seems to be that they don't. In all the years I have spent here, I have never, ever encountered anything that gave me the impression that the country of my birth is hated. Even less me personally as an on-the-spot representative of my country. When you think about them, the above expressions tend to support this view: if you call someone 'our best enemy' it would seem to suggest that there are feelings involved that are considerably warmer than pure hate. Also, the term 'hereditary enemy' makes me think of a long-standing feud between two families who don't get on because of something that happened centuries before, but no one can actually remember what it is they are squabbling about. It would seem that the French and English are brought up to believe that they shouldn't get on, but can't really explain why.

Of course, the fact that the English and the French have spent a high proportion of the past thousand years being at war with each other must leave some kind of scars or, at least, have an effect on their relationship. But, these scars generally only make themselves known during sporting occasions. There aren't really any French equivalents of British tabloid newspapers and, even if there were,

I can't see them coming up with the sort of derogatory, xenophobic headlines for which ours are so well known, particularly when reporting sporting events involving French players.

Incidentally, I had wanted to give a clear figure for the number of years the English and French have been at war. Unfortunately, it is almost impossible to do this because, even when the two countries weren't officially at war, they weren't exactly at peace either. The Hundred Years War is a good example – it lasted from 1337 to 1453 but included several periods where no actual fighting took place, but where peace hadn't been officially declared either.

L'ENTENTE CORDIALE

It is often imagined that this famous agreement in some way formalized a happy and cordial relationship that was supposedly enjoyed at some point in history by the UK and France. In fact it was more a way of agreeing not to step on each other's toes in key places around the world along the lines of, 'You play over there, we'll play over here, and nobody shall play in the middle.'

The Entente was a series of agreements signed as recently as 1904 and included, for example, an undertaking by Britain to allow the French to 'preserve order and provide assistance' in their colony of Morocco. In return the French agreed not to obstruct British actions in Egypt. Other clauses covered a series of other territories in which one or other of the parties had an interest. Thus, the document ensured that each country was free to develop and enjoy its empire without hindrance by the other party.

And that's as cordial as it got.

DONNER DU SANG

A century after the famous Entente, things can still occasionally get a bit strained between the two nations. This came to light when I went to try to give blood at work the other day.

Giving blood in France is particularly rewarding as not only do you feel virtuous afterwards, you also feel very full. This is because, when you have finished, there is no question of being led to a camp bed and being given a cup of tea and a couple of Rich Tea biscuits. In France, once you have recovered a bit, you are led to a table that is arrayed with a veritable feast including croissants, baguettes, ham, saucisson, pickles and tomatoes and even, at one company I worked for, carafes of red wine.

Thus, it was with an optimistically rumbling stomach that I went along to the most recent session as soon as I got to work.

However, it seemed that since I had last given blood, the procedures had changed. Before I could get near the nurse, even less the food table, I had to go and have an interview with a very serious-looking doctor during which I was asked a series of increasingly personal questions. These included:

- Did I weigh less than 50 kg?
- Had I had a baby in the past six months?
- Was I currently taking antibiotics?
- Had I recently had a tooth out?
- Had I recently had a blood transfusion?

OK, I wasn't asked the baby question (it is reserved for women, apparently) but I happily answered 'No' to all the others.

The doctor then turned to the second page of the questionnaire:

- Had I visited a malarial country in the past six months?
- Had I recently had a body piercing?
- Did I take intravenous drugs?
- Had I had unprotected sex with a new partner in the past four months?

With each question, and my increasingly ashamed '*Non*', I felt more and more aware of just how dull and run of the mill my life actually is.

But there was one last question. It turned out to be the real killer:

- Have you spent more than a total of one year in the UK between the years 1980 and 1996?

The fact that I had done just that put an end to my blood-donating career in France. It seems that this is all to do with mad cow disease, which can apparently lurk in your blood and be transmitted to others by blood transfusion.

Being British in France is never something to be taken lightly.

HOW THE BRITISH ARE SEEN GENERALLY

If you were to ask a group of British people what a typical French person is like, you would probably be treated to a selection of stereotypes including some or all of the following:

They wear stripy T-shirts, berets and strings of onions around their necks. The women are incredibly stylish. The men often have comic moustaches. They drink lots of wine. They eat food laced with garlic as well as all sorts of unmentionable things including frogs. They spend a lot of their time in cafés. They are obsessed with sex. They think Jacques Tati is funny. And they all have mistresses (or lovers).

We all know this, so it must be true.

But the one really peculiar thing about French people is that they have no idea of how they should dress up at a British fancy dress party to make clear that they are typically French. If you ask them what they would wear they get it all wrong. When you tell them the correct answer they are shocked, especially when you get to the bit about the onions.

Nevertheless, if you were to ask a French person what a typical British person is like, the answers would be as illuminating as the British ones concerning the French.

For a start, they know we eat pudding. Unfortunately, they have no real idea what it is.

To say that the French don't think much of British food would be a splendid example of understatement. The only tactic that seems to work when a French person starts insulting British cooking is to say that you don't think such an easy target is worthy of them. While they are delighting in the thought of this, you can get the conversation back on to sex where it belongs.

The alarming dishes that the British are known to eat include: overcooked roast lamb with mint sauce; baked beans; vividly coloured jelly; something called 'kidney pie' and, of course, *'le pudding'*. What is not clear in the French mind is whether the pudding in question is a main dish – possibly something like kidney pie – or some horrid dessert like Christmas pudding. But this is of no real importance because they have no intention of having anything to do with it, whatever it is, because they *know* how awful it is. There is a variant of overcooked roast lamb which is also fervently believed to be popular in the UK. This is 'gigot bouilli', or boiled lamb. Some friends were invited to supper by their neighbours, who, keen to make their new English acquaintances feel at home, served them boiled lamb. It was, apparently, indescribably awful.

L'HEURE DU THÉ

Then there is the question of tea.

The first weeks in my new French job were filled with such drama and incomprehension that I didn't have time to study what was going on around me. After a while I was able to notice that, towards the end of the afternoon, various new colleagues seemed to be hovering by my open door with interrogative expressions on their faces. When I finally plucked up the courage to ask what they were waiting for they politely pointed out that it was five o'clock. Pushing for further details revealed the fact that everyone knows that the British have *le five o'clock tea* and they wanted to see what it involved. The fact that I hadn't been having afternoon tea was clearly a huge disappointment to them. So, in a spirit of trans-Channel cooperation, I dutifully turned up the following day with a small teapot and matching cup and saucer that I had inherited from my great-aunt. This was very well received indeed. The only problem was that I tended to have tea as and when I felt like it but rarely at precisely five o'clock. This was a lapse that my colleagues viewed with deep suspicion.

We shall gloss over *le fog londonien* – no French people ever go to London because, as it is always foggy, you can't see anything – and *le chapeau melon* – the bowler hat that, inexplicably, I never wear to work – and consider some British character traits as perceived by the French.

LE FLEGME BRITANNIQUE

While the English are famously known to be perfidious, the British as a whole are phlegmatic. This is witnessed by a well-known term, *le flegme britannique*. I have just looked up the word *flegme* and found that it is a synonym for *non-émotif, froideur impassibilité* and *placidité*. This is odd because if you think of the various British people who feature on the world's stage – sportsmen, sports fans, rock stars, politicians – few of them can be summed up by words like phlegmatic, non-emotive, placid or cool. Nevertheless, the French happily stick to their beliefs on this point. When, years ago, I completely lost my temper for the first time in the middle of a meeting and started yelling furiously at someone, my colleagues, visibly shaken, took shelter beneath the table. But they didn't forsake the *flegme britannique* view: they just reassured each other that I had briefly *perdu mon flegme*, sure in the knowledge that normal service would shortly be resumed.

And then there is the matter of fair play. I always think that, rather than viewing this as a clue to the British way of doing things, the fact that there is no French term for the concept in question gives a better idea of the French character. The characteristic in question is known as *le fair play*. Of course, this term is only ever used about people from countries other than France.

LE SENS DE L'HUMOUR
BRITANNIQUE

The one thing that really causes problems for the British when they visit France is their sense of humour.

It never occurred to me that my sense of humour could be the source of such a fuss. The basic problem is my own fault: I am particularly British when it comes to jokes. When I say something that I think is funny, I leave the job of laughing at what I have said exclusively to the listener. After all, I know that my remark was funny – I said it – so *I* don't need to laugh. The other person laughs if and when they decide that what I have just said is amusing. Thus, each person has a clearly defined role to play in the situation: I, to be funny, and the other person to laugh at what has been said. People like me are rare in France and are viewed with suspicion. They are described as being *pince sans rire*, which more or less means 'deadpan'.

In France the roles should overlap. The listener laughs in the normal way – assuming they find whatever it is funny. But the listener isn't the only one. The person making the funny remark wants to participate in the joke too so as to enjoy it to the full with the listener. They therefore laugh as well, either at the end, or, more probably, all the way through whatever it is they are saying. Thus, funny remarks are a source of much mirth for all those taking part.

I remember my first witticism all too painfully. At the time my new colleagues still hadn't come to terms with the full extent of my Britishness in the same way as I hadn't grasped the full extent of the French language. We were all having a particularly pleasant lunch and I had had a couple of glasses of wine with the meal because I was feeling uncharacteristically extravagant and was thus on the way to the happy state of being *en pleine forme*. Something in the conversation caught my attention and I was suddenly aware that not only had I thought of a brilliant and funny remark to make but, almost inexplicably, I actually knew all the words that I needed to do so. So I said it. The only problem was that I didn't laugh when I said it. Not only that, but because my poor brain was doing its best to make me pronounce all the right words in the correct order, it had no strength left to worry about intonation. So the remark came out in correct French but in a completely flat tone, totally unsuited for humour in any language. And what's more I didn't laugh.

My French companions were thus faced with their strange new colleague saying something deadpan, tonelessly and with his odd accent. They thought about it all and found it amusing, but they could see that I wasn't laughing. The inescapable conclusion was that I hadn't realized that what I had said was actually funny. Under the circumstances, there was only one thing they could do: carefully explain my own joke back to me. After looking at the others, apparently for support, one of them leant forward and said kindly, in the voice of one explaining the Internet to an old-age pensioner, '*Écoute, Charles, c'est marrant parce que ce que tu viens de dire peut-être drôle*' – it's funny you know because what you have just said could be quite amusing. Desperate affirmations that I not only knew it was funny, but that it was exactly what I had been trying to achieve, fell on deaf ears.

This leads us to another potential source of confusion: if a French person tells you a joke and you understand it, it is vital to laugh whether you actually find the joke funny or not. If you understand the joke, don't think it funny and so don't laugh, the person telling the story will automatically assume that you haven't laughed because you haven't understood. They will therefore take the only action they can envisage which is to explain the joke to you, slowly and very painfully. You can protest all you like that you have understood their rotten joke but didn't think it merited a laugh, but it won't do any good. They cracked the joke, they know it was funny but you didn't laugh. The only possible conclusion is that you didn't understand it.

LES VOYAGES EN ANGLETERRE

Only one thing is worse than having a French person explain their rotten joke to you and that is having to suffer their stories about their dreadful exchange trips to Britain.

Even when I used to come to France on holiday, things could get a bit tedious. Inès's family, their friends and even people I barely knew were apparently quite convinced that I wanted to hear their generally unflattering comments about the Queen's hat, the shortcomings of British food and the rotten holidays they had spent in the UK as children. But by far the most tedious were those who had been on a foreign exchange with a British child during their schooldays. These people would feel it necessary to describe to me at great length how they had spent long, harrowing weeks living with the British family from hell. This mean and cruel family always seemed to have lived in the ugliest house in the world, usually jammed between a motorway and a cement works. All members of the household, young and old, spent every evening drinking beer in front of the TV. When it came to mealtimes, the mother of the house, who was invariably large and unpleasant, force-fed them baked beans on toast three times a day. Often, they would have me believe, with jelly on the top. And what's more, it was all my fault.

17. Et, pour conclure . . .
– a few final thoughts

I often hear people complain that, while they know a bit of French, no one in France ever seems to understand them when they try to use it. It seems to me that there is a very good reason for this: they don't speak clearly enough.

Everyone knows a few words of some foreign language or other. My entire knowledge of Dutch, for example, is limited to 'Please give me your paw.' Whenever I used to try to use this (obviously on the rare occasions that I came face to face with a friendly looking Dutch dog) I would become embarrassed and mumble the phrase while laughing nervously. And what happened? Nothing. I had failed to speak clearly and so the dog had no chance of understanding me.

Long years spent in France have since taught me one important thing: your chances of being understood, however little French you speak, are vastly improved if you don't get embarrassed, don't giggle or mumble but speak slowly and clearly. I have shared this theory on many occasions with my family.

My theory was proved, at least to my satisfaction, when we went to Amsterdam a while ago. My daughter's knowledge of Dutch inexplicably comprises the declaration, 'I am a lettuce.' You would reasonably imagine that this is far less useful than being able to ask dogs for their paws. Not a bit of it. On seeing the grubbiest coffee shop that we had passed all day, she strode in, marched up to the bar and slowly and clearly expressed her belief that she was a lettuce. The barman not only understood what she had said, he was so impressed that he shook her hand and gave her a packet of marijuana seeds.

Conclusive stuff, I am sure you will agree.

Thus, however limited your knowledge of French, take a deep breath, calm yourself and do your best to pronounce whatever you want to say slowly and clearly.

I wanted to finish the book on a note of optimism, some example of how, after all these years in France, I have to some degree become assimilated. Unfortunately, I can't think of a suitable example, or even of any example whatsoever. This is quite disturbing because it makes me wonder if, despite all my efforts, I haven't been assimilated in France at all. Perhaps it's too late now.

For want of a more positive example, I thought I would describe what happened the last time we went on a trip to England. We have a French car and, not surprisingly, it has French number plates. After a particularly long and tiring day's travel across a large swathe of the UK, we came to a junction where the lane turning left – where we wanted to go – was filled with a long line of patiently waiting cars, while the lane turning right was more or less empty. Long years in France have clearly taken their toll because, without a second's thought, I pulled out, shot down the right-hand lane and, as I got to the end, barged back into the left-hand lane just as the lights were changing. This, understandably, was not well received: I was treated to a fanfare of hooting and much angry gesturing. This left me relatively indifferent as, like anybody else who drives in France, I get hooted and gestured at all the time, occasionally for good reason. The thing that hurt, and it really hurt, was when the driver of the car I'd pushed in front of wound down his window and bellowed out the worst insult he could think of:

'Froggy bastard!'

Index

If you liked this book, then you'll love...

Pardon My French

Unleash Your Inner Gaul

Charles Timoney

'If you use the words and phrases here you'll be so convincing, French people will talk very fast to you ... this book may be too good!'
Simon Hoggart

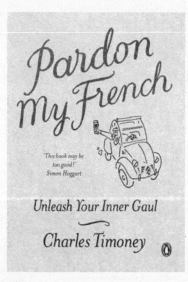

Pardon My French, Charles Timoney's first foray into the Gallic way of life, explores everyday life in France, from eating and drinking to travel and negotiating the workplace. Highly entertaining *and* useful, it will help you avoid the pitfalls and potential embarrassments of speaking French in France.

Immerse yourself in the delights of French food and drink in this excerpt from *Pardon My French* and discover why you shouldn't be concerned if someone asks you for a duck in a café, why you might want a sword if you're going celebrating, and how to navigate through France using just a *pain au chocolat*...

Excerpt from **Pardon My French**

DRINKS AND CAFÉS

Apéro *Apéro* is the familiar form of the word 'apéritif' and is definitely an important one to learn early on. With luck, you can encounter 'un *apéro*' either at the office or at home. At work, people treat their colleagues to an aperitif before a meal to celebrate the birth of a baby, or buying a new car, or to announce a change of job. I have fond memories of sitting down for lunch with colleagues, whereupon one would rub his hands together with delight and cry, 'Allez! C'est moi qui vous offre l'*apéro* aujourd'hui!' before going on to announce some especially good news. We also had a system whereby, if you lost a bet, you had to pay for the *apéros* for everyone. You can of course have aperitifs away from the office, whether before a meal at home with friends or at a restaurant. Inviting someone for an *apéro* or, more correctly, inviting them to 'venir prendre l'apéritif' is a pleasant and simpler alternative to inviting them to supper. Depending on how much food is served, an aperitif can last anywhere from an hour to all evening. The key element of decent *apéros* is good sparkling wine, preferably champagne, in generous quantities. The ultimate *apéro*, which can rival a meal, is something called an 'apéritif dinatoire'. If you get invited to such an *apéro* you can expect the drinks to be accompanied by several types of hot food and there should even be something sweet at the end.

Bière On one of my first forays into a pub with friends at the tender age of sixteen, my friend Paul called for 'Half a pint of beer, please.' This was met with hoots of derision from the landlord as, of course, in the UK you have to specify which sort of beer – bitter, brown ale, mild, etc. – you want. For once, things in France are simpler. You can go into a French bar and order 'Une *bière*, s'il vous plaît' without running the risk of being humiliated. The barman or waiter will generally ask for details, suggesting 'une pression', which means draught beer, or naming a few bottled beers for you to choose from. Experience teaches you that the list tends to start with the cheapest and work upwards. You can speed things up by calling at the outset for 'un demi', which will lead to the barman giving you a glass of draught beer straight away. 'Un demi' used to mean half a litre but now refers to 25cc or a quarter of a litre. Occasionally, you still hear older men in bars calling for 'un bock' when they don't want to drink a whole 'demi'. 'Un bock' is a wineglassful of beer, roughly half the quantity of a 'demi'. I don't know anyone who drinks 'bocks' as there is barely enough for a single swallow.

Canard First of all, you should never offer a French person granulated sugar with their coffee. If they are very polite, they will be visibly shocked; if they are not, they will react as though you are trying to poison them. Only sugar lumps should ever be offered with coffee. Having established this, you have discovered yet another of the many excellent reasons for going to France: dunking sugar lumps in coffee is absolutely divine. Dunking a sugar lump, preferably a large, oblong one, in a cup of strong black coffee is known as 'faire un *canard*' ('*canard*', as you know, usually means duck). When a group of people are together having coffee, it is quite common for a person who hasn't ordered one to pick up a sugar lump, lean over towards someone else's and ask, 'Je peux faire un *canard*?' They thus get a kick of sugary caffeine without having to drink a whole cup.

Champagne *Champagne* is sufficiently important in France to merit two special verbs to cover opening it and drinking it. For a start, you don't just say, 'On va boire du *champagne*,' because it would make it sound about as festive as drinking tap water. When people mean drinking generous quantities of *champagne*, they use the verb 'sabler' as, for example, 'Ce soir, on va sabler le *champagne*.' 'Sabler' doesn't mean open nor yet just drink; it means to drink a good lot of champagne on a festive occasion. There is also a really good word for opening a bottle of *champagne*. This is 'sabrer'. Even though the words look similar, they are quite different. 'Sabrer' literally means to cut with a sabre. Thus 'sabrer le *champagne*' means to whack the neck of the bottle with a sabre and so dispense with all that fiddling with the twisted wires. It is still used, even when no one is intending to get out their sword. The term apparently dates from one of the occupations of France by the Germans in the nineteenth century. Invading troops found themselves in the Champagne region and seem to have put their cavalry sabres to good use when liberating the contents of various cellars.

Coca The manufacturers of Coca-Cola apparently pride themselves that their product is the only one on the planet that has two world-famous names for it: Coca-Cola and Coke. In fact, they have reason to feel even more proud because the common word for their product in France is neither Coca-Cola nor Coke but simply *Coca*. Going into a French bar and ordering 'un Coke' will generally result in the barman repeating the order but with the words 'un *Coca*'. Ordering 'un *Coca*' – provided that's what you want! – is a good way of showing that you are starting to get the hang of things.

Coup This word literally means a blow or a knock and this explains why the first time someone offered me one in a bar, I took a quick step backwards. In fact, 'un *coup* à boire' is a drink. When you suggest going for a drink to someone you might say, 'Je t'offre un *coup* à boire?', or possibly 'Je te paie un *coup*?', which is somewhat less chic. (As a general rule, when treating someone to something, it is preferable to use 'offrir' rather than 'payer'.) Encouraging someone to come for a drink might involve saying, 'Allez! On va boire un *coup*?' and heading off purposefully towards the bar. As far as I can tell, *coup* applies only to alcoholic drinks; offering someone a soft drink would be phrased differently, for example, 'Tu veux boire quelque chose?' You can specify that the drink in question is red or white wine simply by adding on the appropriate colour. A glass of red wine is 'un *coup* de rouge', but calling it that does not say much for the quality of wine on offer. Finally, if you overdo your consumption of *coups* you are said to have 'bu un *coup* en trop' or more colourfully 'avoir un *coup* dans le nez'.

Deux . . . deux If you listen carefully the next time you go to a café or a brasserie, you will hear the double coffee order. Assuming it is not the sort of place where the waiter himself makes the coffee, he will call the order to the barman who will then get it ready and set the cups on the bar. What is interesting is that the waiter repeats the number of coffees ordered just after the word 'cafés'. Thus, instead of calling out, 'Deux cafés!', the waiter in fact shouts, '*Deux* cafés . . . *deux*!' This is presumably intended to give the barman a second or so to jerk himself from his reverie and think, 'What? Did someone call for coffee? But how many did he want?', whereupon he hears the second 'deux' right on cue. Some waiters do the double order for any drinks, shouting out, 'Trois Ricards . . . trois!' This seems to work only for orders of a single sort of drink. Composite orders like '*deux* pressions . . . *deux*, et un Ricard' would sound silly.

Eau de source Knowing about this earlier would have saved us money. Arriving in France, one of the first things you become aware of is the French obsession with mineral water. Plastic bottles of all shapes and sizes feature strongly on tables and desks across the land. At first sight, all the bottles have famous labels – Évian, Vittel, Volvic and Contrex being the most popular. These actually all taste different, the easiest to spot being Contrex, which tastes more strongly of minerals than any of the others. Such branded mineral waters are, however, surprisingly expensive, even when bought in bulk. Then came the happy day when we discovered that a basically similar product existed which sold at a fraction of the cost of the famous brands. This is generically labelled spring water or *eau de source*. Spring water comes in plain, cheap, litre-and-a-half bottles, or can be bought even more cheaply in huge plastic containers which hold several litres. The only problem with these is getting them home. At least lifting them up to pour the water is not a problem as they have a handy tap on the bottom. There used to be (and perhaps there still is) a spot in rue de la Pompe in Paris where spring water was available from a public tap. You would see people queuing with loads of empty mineral water bottles waiting to fill them up for free.

Pot A drinks party at work to celebrate a wedding, a birth or some other happy domestic event is commonly known as 'un *pot*'. People also do 'un *pot*' on their last day at work before retiring or before leaving for a new job. When you learn that a colleague has handed in his notice, is about to get married or has just produced an heir, someone will invariably ask, 'Quand est-ce qu'il fait son *pot*?', sure in the knowledge that a *pot* will be organized. In the days preceeding the *pot*, a collection goes round for a present, a procedure known as 'faire passer une enveloppe'.

Pourboire The French word for tip, which I include because any visitor to France should be aware that in French restaurants and bars, the tip is already included. In the old days, when you called for the bill, the waitress would add up all the things that you had ordered and then, in the blink of an eye, add on 15 per cent service charge. Now the price of each item shown on a menu already includes the tip. If you look at the bottom of a menu, it should say, in extremely small print, 'Service 15% inclus' or some such. Hard as it may be to believe, I have seen menus in tourist restaurants where this phrase has been inadvertently mistranslated as 'Service not included'. How they came to make a mistake like that is beyond me! In bars, if the barman or the waiter has been friendly, it is customary to leave a few centimes, despite the fact that you have in fact already tipped. The only problem with the tip being included – and at 15 per cent it can be a sizeable sum – is that you can't get out of paying it even if the service or the food has been awful. In the old days, if things were not satisfactory, you would simply not leave a tip at all. It is not clear whether the enforced inclusion of the service charge has led to better or worse service in restaurants and bars.

Zinc *Zinc* can be used to refer to a bar or to an aircraft, and in either sense should be pronounced more like 'zaing' than *zinc*.

Before the bars of French bistrots came to be covered in tiles, synthetic materials or imitation marble, the counter was made out of a sheet of zinc. Over the years, the metal surface became scratched and battered, giving the top of the bar a wonderful silvery patina. People would describe having had a drink 'sur le *zinc*' rather than 'au comptoir', an expression which is still common, even though zinc-topped bars no longer are.

BREAD AND CAKES

Baguette Of course you know what this is, and so did I when I first arrived in France. What I didn't know was that you don't have to buy the whole thing. Buying a whole *baguette* and then not eating all of it in the course of the day, used to annoy me intensely because the bread was stale by the next morning. Until the day when I heard someone ask for 'une demi-*baguette*' at my local BOULANGERIE. Half a *baguette* was handed over without a raised eyebrow. Indeed, I now realize that quite a few people, especially single people, regularly buy only half. You can even buy two halves in the course of one day and thus enjoy fresh bread both for breakfast and in the evening. There is more: experts who particularly like a crusty, or a less crusty, *baguette* go on to request one that is 'bien cuite' – well done – or 'pas trop cuite' – not too crusty. Another unexpected variant is offered by asking for something called 'une *baguette* moulée'. This is a loaf which has been baked in a shaped baking tray, rather than on a flat plate, and thus has a lower half that is softer and less crusty. All this should enable you to broaden your bread-buying horizons enormously.

Boulangerie/pâtisserie Setting off to buy bread in France can leave you with a choice between two shops, both apparently selling bread, but one labelled *Boulangerie*, while the other has a sign saying *Pâtisserie*. What is the difference? And which one should you choose? 'Une *boulangerie*' is a baker's shop. In it you should expect to find various types of bread, assorted PAINS AU CHOCO-LAT, croissants and the like, collectively known as 'viennoiseries', and also a few nice cakes, which will probably be displayed in the shop window. 'Une *pâtisserie*' is an up-market *boulangerie*. It will have a similar range of breads and 'viennoiseries' but will offer a far broader choice of delicious cakes of all shapes and sizes, some of which will be very expensive indeed. If you just want bread, or are on a limited budget, it is probably a good idea to opt for a *boulangerie* so that you won't be tempted by the amazing cakes in the *pâtisserie*. This is especially good advice at the weekend when there are queues of people waiting for their cakes and 'tartes' to be wrapped up. Some bakers who are particularly proud of their bread-making will label themselves '*boulangerie* artisanale'. An 'artisan' is a craftsman.

Et avec ceci? This is the cry of bakers, greengrocers and butchers or any stallholder in a French market. You ask for your BAGUETTE, or a dozen spicy sausages called merguez, or a kilo of potatoes and the seller, once he has handed you your order, nicely wrapped up, will enquire, '*Et avec ceci?*' The question literally means And with this . . . ? and is intended to check whether you need anything else. Even if you have already asked for everything you want, the question has a secondary, and more important, function: to encourage you to look at the various wares before you and spot something you hadn't planned on buying. And so increase the value of the sale. Nine times out of ten you have no further purchase to make and thus will reply firmly, 'Ça sera tout, merci' – that will be all, thanks. Oddly enough, while the salesperson will have greeted you, and possibly checked some aspect of your order, in a perfectly normal voice, the all-important question 'Et avec ceci . . . ?' will invariably be asked in a completely different, and generally irritating and ingratiating, tone. The whiny, subservient tone annoys me so much that I will reply, 'Ça sera tout, merci' even if I have actually thought of something else I need. Those unfamiliar with the question have been known to misunderstand it entirely, notably one local English resident who was asked it each time he went to the butcher's. He thought he was being asked 'Et avec saucisses?', and assumed that the butcher was enquiring whether he also wanted some sausages. His reply of 'Non merci, je n'en veux pas' must have been perplexing to the poor chap.

Gâteau A word that has caused me great disappointment over the years. The problem arose because I was taught it was the French for cake – a birthday cake, for example, being 'un *gâteau* d'anniversaire'. Came the first time at a friend's house that we were asked 'Vous voulez des *gâteaux*?' Images arose of chocolate cake, or some delicious fruit affair stuffed with cream. I accepted enthusiastically, only to see my host return with a plate of plain biscuits. It seems that *gâteaux* is a synonym for biscuits, the words being apparently interchangeable. If you are faced with an offer of a *gâteau*, the only clues you will have to work out what this means is that either it will be in the plural – 'des *gâteaux*' – in which case it is unlikely that there will be several cakes on offer, or they will be specified as being 'des petits *gâteaux*'. Were real cakes being offered, then small ones would be referred to as 'pâtisseries' and not 'petits *gâteaux*'. Old-fashioned, hard biscuits are generally called '*gâteaux* secs'. Obviously, if something is being referred to as 'sec' – dry – it is a good indication that it will not be a rich chocolate cake. There are also salty nibbles that are served with an APÉRO and are called '*gâteaux* apéritifs' or '*gâteaux* salés'. You really have to be on your guard whenever the word *gâteau* crops up in order to avoid being as disappointed as I was!

Pain au chocolat/chocolatine
This is an example of something whose name changes according to where in France you order it. In Paris and in most of northern France, the delicious, flaky, buttery pastry roll with a length of chocolate inside it which revives you, in time of need, at any hour of the day, is known as a *pain au chocolat*. Once you head south and get below about the level of Bordeaux, if you go into a local baker and call for a *pain au chocolat*, you will be met with incomprehension. In the south, it is called a *chocolatine*. I have been known, when on holiday, to rush into the first bakery I see and order one, merely for the joy of using the word. Asking for a *chocolatine* in northern France will, of course, be met with similar incomprehension. If you get lost on the way to the south of France, and want to work out roughly where you are, ordering a *pain au chocolat* may be a means of finding out how far south you have actually travelled.

Tartine
The French have two words for bread-based snack foods. One is SANDWICH, the other is *tartine*, which describes a single piece of bread on which is laid or spread whatever you fancy. *Tartines* do not necessarily have to have anything other than butter on them. Indeed, the ideal accompaniment to a cup of coffee in a bar early in the morning is 'une *tartine* beurrée' or two. This is a

piece of BAGUETTE, cut lengthways and generously buttered. Dipped into your coffee, it becomes quite simply delicious. You can have *tartines* with jam or cheese, or anything else you want. If the bread you have is a bit stale, you can grill it and make a '*tartine* grillée'.

PENGUIN POCKET REFERENCE

THE PENGUIN POCKET FRENCH DICTIONARY
ROSALIND FERGUSSON

The Penguin Pocket French Dictionary is an invaluable and handy wordfinder for students and travellers alike. Covering both English–French and French–English, it offers clear definitions in an easy-to-use format, ensuring that you find the word you need quickly and efficiently.

- Includes over 35,000 entries

- Gives entry-by-entry guidance on pronunciation

- Lists irregular verbs in both languages

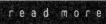
PENGUIN REFERENCE

THE MEANING OF TINGO
ADAM JACOT DE BOINOD

Did you know that the Albanians have twenty-seven words for moustache?

Or that in Hungary pigs go röf-röf-röf?

Or that tingo is an Easter Island word meaning 'to borrow things from a friend's house one by one until there's nothing left'?

Here are the most weird and wonderful words from all around the world, showing the curious ways different countries talk about food, emotions, animals and even facial hair – as well as many things you hadn't even realized had words to describe them …

'A book no well-stocked bookshelf, cistern-top or handbag should be without'
Stephen Fry

'A luscious list of linguistic one-liners' *Daily Express*

ANNE FADIMAN

EX LIBRIS
ANNE FADIMAN

'Witty, enchanting and supremely well written' Robert McCrum, *Observer*

This witty collection of essays recounts a lifelong love affair with books and language. For Fadiman, as for many passionate readers, the books she loves have become chapters in her own life story.

Writing with remarkable grace, she revives the tradition of the well-crafted personal essay, moving easily from anecdotes about Coleridge and Orwell to tales of her own pathologically literary family. As someone who played at blocks with her father's 22-volume set of Trollope ('My Ancestral Castles') and who only really considered herself married when she and her husband had merged collections ('Marrying Libraries'), she is exquisitely well equipped to expand upon the art of inscriptions, the perverse pleasures of compulsive proof-reading, the allure of long words, and the satisfactions of reading out loud. There is even a foray into pure literary gluttony – Charles Lamb liked buttered muffin crumbs between the leaves, and Fadiman knows of more than one reader who literally consumes page corners.

Perfectly balanced between humour and erudition, *Ex Libris* establishes Fadiman as one of the world's finest contemporary essayists.

'*Ex Libris* will provide enjoyable moments of recognition for all book obsessives' Alain de Botton

Penguin Language

THE STORIES OF ENGLISH
DAVID CRYSTAL

How did a language originally spoken by a few thousand Anglo-Saxons become one used by more than 1,500 million people? How have all the different versions of English evolved and changed? In this compelling global tour, David Crystal turns the traditional view of the history of the language on its head and tells the *real* stories of English that have never before been fully told.

'A spirited celebration . . . Crystal gives the story of English a new plot' *Guardian*

'Rejoices in dialects, argots and cants . . . enlightening – in a word, excellent' *Sunday Times*

'An exhilarating read . . . Crystal is a sort of latter-day Johnson' *The Times Higher Education Supplement*

'*The Stories of English* reads like an adventure story. Which, of course, it is' Roger McGough

'A marvellous book . . . for anyone who loves the English language(s) it will be a treasure-house' Philip Pullman

PENGUIN NATURAL HISTORY

HATFIELD'S HERBAL
GABRIELLE HATFIELD

From ivy-wreathed buildings to the dandelions growing through the cracks between paving stones, we are surrounded by a wealth of native plants.

In the past they were a hugely valued resource: magical, mystical and medical. When Charles I visited Staffordshire his chamberlain wrote to the local sheriff asking him to ensure that no fern should be burnt or cut during the king's visit, so that the weather would be fine. Puppies were once fed daisy flowers in milk to keep them small while children wore daisy chains to protect against fairy kidnapping.

Packed with stories and memorable information, this book is the highly personal, very readable result of a lifetime spent researching folk cures and the science behind them. Outlining the history and uses of over 150 British plants, *Hatfield's Herbal* offers a fascinating history of what life was once like, a beautifully illustrated, evocative guide to our native plants and a passionate argument for why we should better appreciate the riches we already have.

'Hatfield, a contemporary botanist and plant historian, covers remedies from agrimony to yew and the history of their use' *Sunday Times*, Books of the Year

He just wanted a decent book to read ...

Not too much to ask, is it? It was in 1935 when Allen Lane, Managing Director of Bodley Head Publishers, stood on a platform at Exeter railway station looking for something good to read on his journey back to London. His choice was limited to popular magazines and poor-quality paperbacks – the same choice faced every day by the vast majority of readers, few of whom could afford hardbacks. Lane's disappointment and subsequent anger at the range of books generally available led him to found a company – and change the world.

'We believed in the existence in this country of a vast reading public for intelligent books at a low price, and staked everything on it'
Sir Allen Lane, 1902–1970, founder of Penguin Books

The quality paperback had arrived – and not just in bookshops. Lane was adamant that his Penguins should appear in chain stores and tobacconists, and should cost no more than a packet of cigarettes.

Reading habits (and cigarette prices) have changed since 1935, but Penguin still believes in publishing the best books for everybody to enjoy. We still believe that good design costs no more than bad design, and we still believe that quality books published passionately and responsibly make the world a better place.

So wherever you see the little bird – whether it's on a piece of prize-winning literary fiction or a celebrity autobiography, political tour de force or historical masterpiece, a serial-killer thriller, reference book, world classic or a piece of pure escapism – you can bet that it represents the very best that the genre has to offer.

Whatever you like to read – trust Penguin.